Do the right thing

The practical, jargon-free guide to
corporate social responsibility

Stephen Asbury and Richard Ball

Published 2009

© Stephen Asbury and Richard Ball 2009
Printed in England by the Lavenham Press Limited

ISBN-13: 978 0 901357 42 7

Published by IOSH Services Ltd
The Grange
Highfield Drive
Wigston
Leicestershire
LE18 1NN
UK
t +44 (0)116 257 3100
f +44 (0)116 257 3101
www.iosh.co.uk

Recycled
Supporting responsible use
of forest resources
www.fsc.org   Cert no. SGS-COC-004865
© 1996 Forest Stewardship Council

The pages of this book are printed on 100 per cent recycled paper. The cover uses 80 per cent recycled card and is protected by a biodegradable gloss laminate.

Contents

Foreword

Sustainability is an enormous opportunity for business. It allows us to create a new, deeper relationship with our customers, employees and suppliers, to become more efficient and cut our cost base, to develop new business opportunities and to create stability and security in our supply chains.

But these opportunities will not come to fruition for those who believe that sustainable business is just a continuation of today's model of corporate social responsibility. There is little point in launching a few worthy projects that excite, at one extreme, allegations of 'greenwash' from external stakeholders, and at the other a weary shrug from the finance director.

Success will only come from making sustainability 'how we do business', fully engrained within the day-to-day heartbeat of a company. Not because we ought to keep stakeholders happy, but because we want to because it brings us business success. And that's why I'm so supportive of the work that IOSH is doing with this book. The great strides that have been made in improving health and safety in business in recent decades, particularly manufacturing, have come from making safety how we do business, not a risk to be tolerated but one where we have 'zero tolerance'. The same commitment, drive and business focus can do the same for sustainability.

Richard S Gillies
Director, Plan A, Marks and Spencer plc

Corporate social responsibility can seem a baffling concept to some, combining as it does ethics and environmental and social values with the business world, understandably concerned with making profit, and sustaining its enterprise into the future. But 'sustainability' applies happily to both – society and business. The best work in corporate social responsibility recognises that these two needs can be balanced, and mutually beneficial. My own work at Age Concern, the Equality and Human Rights Commission and the International Longevity Centre-UK shows that valuing people and their place in society isn't just about 'doing the right thing' – it's about maximising potential for individuals and business.

I welcome this new book from IOSH, designed to bring clarity and understanding to a subject that's critical today, and will become increasingly important in the decades ahead.

Baroness Greengross OBE
Chair, All Party Parliamentary Group on Corporate Responsibility

Sustainable development must no longer be seen as an optional extra – simply put, it makes excellent business sense. I believe that every company must demonstrate improving environmental practices and performance to all their stakeholders. This won't only halt the damage to our environment, but also save on company resources. I am pleased to see our fellow professional body, IOSH, publish this new, highly readable book on corporate social responsibility, which aptly demonstrates how progressive businesses really can reap the full benefits of good environmental stewardship.

Russell Foster
Chief Executive, Institute of Environmental Management and Assessment

It's not enough to talk the environmental message – we have to learn to live by it. We already know through our work that social, environmental and economic issues *can* be balanced and integrated. The result is a win–win – individuals and enterprises prosper, and so do local communities and the global environment. We actively encourage practical steps towards a more sustainable future, which is why we're happy to support IOSH's new action-based book on CSR.

David Nicholls
Chief Executive, Groundwork Leicester and Leicestershire

Acknowledgments

Stephen Asbury

Thank you to my colleagues at Corporate Risk Systems and to our clients. Working with you is always more fun than I expected. Thank you too to our training delegates for showing up, listening to our messages and making 'work' such a pleasure. I'd also like to publicly thank the friends that have shaped my thinking – both at work and in my personal life.

Thank you to Richard, my co-author, for his checks and challenges. You have been a pleasure to write with. Thank you to the team at IOSH for their support in helping develop our script into something which we hope is of value to our readers.

From the first words for this book written in Trinidad, to the closing thoughts penned in Houston, this book has been one more personal adventure. As ever, I thank my late parents Alan and Betty. My family tells me that they would be proud of me.

This book is dedicated to Kimberley, my daughter, and my personal hope for the future.

Richard Ball

This book could not have happened without my wife Tash – thanks for making me strive to go on when I couldn't, and slow down when I could. My interest in the world stems from a chain of individuals who have supported me throughout my life, shaping my ideas and forging my thoughts – thanks for listening to me.

I would like to give special mention to my co-author Stephen. Thanks must also go to our clients for the opportunity to do interesting work that makes a difference, and our course candidates for challenging my ideas.

I'd like to dedicate this book to my children, Macey and Harrison. I strive to make this world a better place for all, but especially you. Go out into the world and enjoy it, but respect its people and its nature.

About the authors

Stephen Asbury MBA FRSA FIEMA CEnv CFIOSH

Stephen Asbury is managing director of Corporate Risk Systems Limited, an international auditing and training organisation. He worked in a variety of commercial risk management roles with Rugby Group plc, BTR plc (now Invensys plc), and GKN plc, before moving into consultancy in 1996 as head of liability consulting with Royal and Sun Alliance Insurance Group plc. After a short spell as a director of Aon, he co-founded Corporate Risk Systems in 1999.

Stephen was RoSPA Safety Professional of the Year (Engineering) in 1995 as a result of his pioneering work on handling employer's liability insurance claims.

Stephen is a Chartered Fellow of IOSH and a Chartered Environmentalist. Since 1998, he has been a member of the IOSH Council of Management, and is currently chair of the IOSH Professional Committee.

In his spare time, he enjoys theatre, scuba diving and F1 motor sport.

Richard Ball PgDip BSc (Hons) MIEMA CMIOSH

Richard Ball is head of environment at Corporate Risk Systems. He has worked on corporate social responsibility (CSR) projects in a wide range of sectors. Richard graduated in environmental management, before starting work in the automotive industry. He then moved into the public sector, working for a statutory organisation supporting young people, charities and voluntary organisations, with facilities management and risk management responsibilities.

Since moving into the consultancy sector, Richard has developed and delivered health and safety, environmental and CSR training courses for organisations including the London Eye, Heathrow Terminal 5, police forces, nightclubs, universities, local authorities and manufacturers. He has contributed to a foundation degree in leadership and management and worked on a variety of consultancy and auditing projects, including CSR.

Richard is environmental protection curriculum adviser for the Chartered Institute of Environmental Health, and is currently working on developing its new range of courses.

In his leisure time he enjoys running and spending time with his young family. He is also a school governor.

Introduction

千里之行，始于足下
(Even the longest journey begins with a single step)
Tao Te Ching (6th century BC)

Our planet, the earth, seems incredibly durable. For the last 4.6 billion years, it's apparently handled everything the universe has thrown at it. Occasional catastrophes have punctuated long periods of stable conditions that are ideal for life, but each time the planet has recovered and continues to support a wealth of life. Today, it provides an ideal home for 2 million or so catalogued species – it's the only place in the universe where life is known to exist.

There are now 6.5 billion human beings on earth and the population is growing at a rate of about 80 million per year. No species has previously dominated our planet in the way that we now do. Is our behaviour changing the conditions we need to survive? Is it sustainable?

Driven by our desire for wealth and our expanding population, we've plundered the earth for its resources – ores, coal, oil, gas and wood. Our hydrocarbon fuels will probably run out in the next 100 years. We know this, and have been investing in wind, wave, solar and biofuel alternatives, as well as nuclear power. But these aren't without their problems. The Chernobyl disaster – so far the only level 7 release on the International Nuclear Event Scale – caused 56 immediate deaths, an estimated 9,000 additional cancer cases and the evacuation and resettlement of over 300,000 people. Biofuels, once hailed as the answer to both climate change and a shortage of fossil fuels, are now implicated in the recent rises in food prices. Can we grow enough crops for food *and* fuel? Or is it a question of distributing wealth more equitably between the continents?

Carbon dioxide levels in the atmosphere are increasing at alarming levels. After years of debate, the environmentalists seem to have won this argument, and we all know that we should reduce our waste, recycle and cut down on our driving. So far, 25 per cent of man-made carbon emissions have been absorbed by the world's forests. But these natural lungs are threatened by the same man-made processes – the need for land to feed and house an expanding population. An area of around 75,000 square kilometres – the size of Austria or South Carolina – is destroyed each year (UN 2005).

But it's not just the environment we're affecting. There's also inequality within our species, exemplified by the historical slave trade, modern sweatshops, child labour and the sex trade. How far are nations and organisations prepared to go to create wealth?

It's not all bad news. Happily, we've developed 'eco-friendly' bullets, grenades and rockets, and carbon-neutral beer. Every time we read a newspaper, watch the television or listen to a politician, we're urged to 'save the earth'. History shows us that species and civilisations come and go, but the earth survives. So perhaps it isn't the earth we should be so worried about – perhaps we should be more worried about saving ourselves.

Corporate social responsibility (CSR) is a powerful tool to help us do this. This book will help and encourage you to get involved – to take the first steps on a long journey. It will take you through the theory and practice of CSR – why it's a good idea, how organisations can implement it and how it'll help them achieve their other goals too. We've also included a chapter on personal social responsibility – or how you can apply the principles of CSR in your personal life. We recognise that any new idea needs thorough testing, so we've summarised the common arguments against CSR in Chapter 7.

To bring the theory to life, we've included several case studies. These use publicly available material and, unless we've said otherwise, are presented here without the knowledge or agreement of the organisations concerned. We've also included a list of 100 CSR actions (see page 129) that will help you start to make a difference.

Scattered through the book are 20 'Test your thinking' exercises to encourage you to think more about CSR and apply the theories in this book to your own organisation. For some of these we've suggested some answers, but elsewhere we've deliberately left them open-ended. This book doesn't provide all the answers! We hope it'll lead you to read more about CSR and delve further into this fascinating topic. All the 'Test your thinking' exercises can be downloaded from www.iosh.co.uk/books.

Throughout the text, we've included web addresses for resources and information we've referred to. Some of these are repeated in the 'Websites to watch' section on page 141. Inevitably, links disappear and text on webpages changes over the lifetime of a printed book. If you find a broken link, take a look at www.iosh.co.uk/books, where we'll post changes where possible.

The highest courage is to dare to be yourself in the face of adversity. Choosing right over wrong, ethics over convenience, and truth over popularity... these are the choices that measure your life. Travel the path of integrity without looking back, for there is never a wrong time to do the right thing.
Attributed to Michael Moore, American film maker

Those who cannot learn from history are doomed to repeat it.
George Santayana, Spanish-American writer (1863–1952)

Chapter 1: CSR in context

"One small step for man, one giant leap for mankind"
Astronaut Neil Armstrong on the surface of the Moon, 20 July 1969

Our home, the planet we call earth, is billions of years old. It has taken a very long time for it to become just right for life to thrive. In the course of just a few generations, we are causing a lot of damage to it, consuming more than our fair share of its resources and exploiting too many of its people. While for most of the earth's life extinction has been a natural phenomenon, we may be at the brink of substantial change. Some experts have estimated that up to half of presently existing species may become extinct by 2100 (Wilson, 2002). We have a lot to do and little time in which to do it. Let's get started…

A short history of the earth

Everything we know, and possibly everything we'll ever know, started 13.7 billion years ago with an event that has become universally known as the 'Big Bang'. The first stars were formed from the hydrogen and helium created at this time. As a result of nuclear reactions, heavier elements were generated that resulted, around 5 billion years ago, in the creation of stars such as our Sun.

Around 4.6 billion years ago, the earth began to form from a cloud of dust, rocks and gas. As it grew, its gravitational field allowed it to retain an atmosphere, including water. A mixture of volcanic activity and bombardment by objects from space altered the atmosphere, creating a mixture of mainly ammonia, methane, water vapour, carbon dioxide and nitrogen.

Life on earth

We can only speculate about how and when life began on earth – perhaps around 4 billion years ago. In the energetic chemistry of the early earth, a molecule (or something else) gained the ability to make copies of itself. This 'magic' molecule is widely known as the 'Original Replicator'. The nature of this molecule is unknown, its function having long since been superseded by life's current replicator, deoxyribonucleic acid (DNA).

Current evidence suggests that the last universal common ancestor lived during the early Archean Eon, perhaps 3.5 billion years ago or earlier. This cell is the ancestor of all cells, and hence of all life on earth. It was probably an early prokaryote, possessing a cell membrane and probably ribosomes, but lacking a nucleus or membrane-bound organelles such as mitochondria or chloroplasts. Like all modern cells, it used DNA as its genetic code, RNA for information transfer and protein synthesis, and enzymes to catalyse reactions.

Life remained unicellular for up to 2.5 billion years. Around 1 billion years ago, the first multi-cellular plants emerged, probably green algae in the oceans. Possibly by around 100 million years later, multi-cellularity had also evolved in animals, probably sponges.

For most of the earth's history, there has been no life on land. The oldest fossils of land fungi and plants date to 480–460 million years ago, though molecular evidence suggests they may have colonised the land earlier than this. The process will have started with plants (probably resembling algae) and fungi growing first at the edges of the water and then out of it. Although these organisms initially stayed close to the water's edge, mutations and variations resulted in further colonisation of this new land environment. When the first animals left the oceans is not precisely known: the oldest clear evidence is of arthropods on land around 450 million years ago, perhaps thriving and becoming better adapted as a result of the vast food source provided by the terrestrial plants.

Four-legged animals evolved from fish around 380 to 375 million years ago, and by 360 million years ago they were spreading across the land. Around 310 million years ago the synapsids (which include mammals) diverged from birds and reptiles.

The most severe extinction event to date took place 250 million years ago, at the boundary of the Permian and Triassic Periods, known as the P–T extinction event. Around 95 per cent of life on earth died out, possibly due to the Siberian Traps volcanic event, the largest eruptions known. But life persevered, and around 230 million years ago, dinosaurs split off from their reptilian ancestors. Another extinction event occurred 200 million years ago, though this spared many of the dinosaurs, and they soon became dominant among the vertebrates. Though some of the mammalian lines began to separate during this period, the mammals at this time were probably all small animals resembling shrews.

The first birds lived around 150 million years ago. Competition with the new birds drove many non-avian birds such as pterosaurs to extinction, and the dinosaurs were probably already in decline for various reasons when, 65 million years ago, an asteroid nine miles wide struck earth just off the Yucatán Peninsula in Mexico, ejecting vast quantities of particulate matter and vapour into the air that occluded sunlight, inhibiting photosynthesis. Most large animals, including the non-avian dinosaurs, became extinct, marking the end of the Cretaceous Period and Mesozoic Era. In the Paleocene Epoch, mammals rapidly diversified, grew larger, and became the dominant vertebrates. A small African ape, *Australopithecus africanus*, which lived around 6 million years ago, was the last animal whose descendants would include both modern humans and their closest relatives, the chimpanzees.

Human history

Humanoid apes of the genus *Homo* have been around for only a tiny fraction of the history of the world that we've just outlined. And of that tiny fraction – around 2 million years – 99 per cent is classified as the Stone Age, during which *Homo sapiens* and other, now extinct, species developed stone tools and the use of fire.

The first humans to show evidence of spirituality were the Neanderthals (generally classified as a separate species, *Homo neanderthalensis*, and with no surviving descendants). Neanderthals buried their dead, often with food or tools beside them. Evidence of more sophisticated beliefs, such as in early cave paintings, appeared 32,000 years ago.

Anatomically modern humans – *Homo sapiens* – are believed to have originated around 200,000–250,000 years ago in Africa. The oldest human fossils date back to around 160,000 years ago, and humans had spread as far as Borneo by 40,000 years ago. By 11,000 years ago, *Homo sapiens* had reached the southern tip of South America, the last of the uninhabited continents apart from Antarctica. Tool use and language continued to improve; interpersonal relationships became more complex.

Throughout more than 90 per cent of its history, *Homo sapiens* lived in small bands as nomadic hunter-gatherers. Language became more complex, the ability to remember and transmit information increased, and ideas could be exchanged and passed down through the generations. Cultural evolution outpaced biological evolution, and history proper began.

The history of the last 10,000 years or so is one of continuous cultural, social and technological development. Yet it wasn't until the end of the 18th century that humans began to develop the technology that allows us to lead our modern lives – and affect the entire planet, for good or ill. Today, we have the power to alter the world's climate and annihilate ourselves with immensely powerful weapons. The figure on the next page lays out the earth's history proportionally – it shows how short humanity's time on earth has been, yet how disproportionate our effects on the planet. We mentioned extinction events early in the planet's history – the major known and likely ones are listed in the table on page 17. Worrying, isn't it?

A proportional
view of the history
of the world

Key:
ya: years ago
mya: millions of
years ago

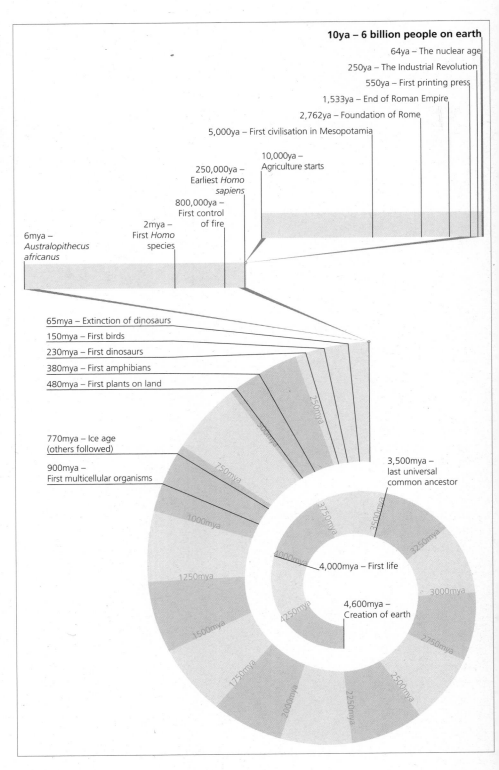

10ya – 6 billion people on earth

64ya – The nuclear age

250ya – The Industrial Revolution

550ya – First printing press

1,533ya – End of Roman Empire

2,762ya – Foundation of Rome

5,000ya – First civilisation in Mesopotamia

10,000ya –
Agriculture starts

250,000ya –
Earliest *Homo
sapiens*

800,000ya –
First control
of fire

2mya –
First *Homo*
species

6mya –
*Australopithecus
africanus*

65mya – Extinction of dinosaurs

150mya – First birds

230mya – First dinosaurs

380mya – First amphibians

480mya – First plants on land

770mya – Ice age
(others followed)

900mya –
First multicellular organisms

3,500mya –
last universal
common ancestor

4,000mya – First life

4,600mya –
Creation of earth

250mya

750mya

1000mya

1250mya

1500mya

1750mya

2000mya

2250mya

2500mya

2750mya

3000mya

3250mya

3500mya

3750mya

4000mya

4250mya

770 million years ago	Ice age caused all the oceans to freeze	Extinction events
488 million years ago	Ice age	
440 million years ago	Ice age	
365 million years ago	Ice age	
250 million years ago	Siberian Traps volcanic event: the largest eruptions in history; known as the P–T extinction event	
65 million years ago	Asteroid nine miles wide hits Mexico; credited with extinction of dinosaurs; the K–T extinction event	
Biblical flood legend	Noah and his family the only human survivors of 150 days of flooding, finally found dry land on the Mountains of Ararat in Turkey	
1991	99.9% of all species that have ever lived are now extinct	
2100	Half of presently existing species extinct?	

Over 250 years since the start of this growth in knowledge, technology, commerce, and the destructiveness of war, development on so many fronts has accelerated, creating the opportunities and perils that now confront the human communities that together inhabit earth. Change has continued, and still continues, at a near exponential pace. We have seen the development (and destruction) of nuclear weapons, stem cell research, mapping the human genome and early endeavours in sustainable energy. At the same time, we have developed huge capacity computers, big advances in medical care, and nanotechnology. Economic globalisation spurred by advances in communication and transport technology has influenced everyday life in many parts of the world. Political, cultural and institutional systems such as democracy, capitalism and environmentalism have all played a part in shaping life on earth as it is today. Major concerns and problems such as disease, war, poverty and global warming have become more pressing, and the world population is increasing. The economies, political affairs and defence of nations around the world have become increasingly intertwined. This globalisation has often produced discord, although increased collaboration has resulted as well.

We'll need the highest level of collaboration we've ever seen if humans are to overcome the current environmental challenges. But with diminishing resources, increasing populations, climate change, epidemic diseases, regional wars and terrorism, this goal seems distant. Are humans bringing life on earth to an end?

Four and a half billion years after the planet's formation, one of earth's life forms broke free of the biosphere. For the first time in history, earth was viewed first-hand from space. Yuri Gagarin was the first human to orbit the earth, in 1957, and 12 years later Neil Armstrong was the first person to step onto the surface of the moon – yet we still can't feed the earth's population.

We urge you, like Neil Armstrong, to take the first 'small step' on this new journey for the human race.

> The current generation has the opportunity to affect the destiny of the human race
> *Professor Michio Kaku, American theoretical physicist*

We have relied on a broad number of sources for Chapter 1, but recommend Wells (1920), Parker (1997), and Spodek (2001) for the main chronology.

Chapter 2: The evolution of CSR

"We could really lose it – ... what we take for granted might not be here for our children"
Al Gore, former US Vice-President and international environmental campaigner

"Symbiotic relationships mean creative partnerships. The Earth is to be seen neither as an ecosystem to be preserved unchanged, nor as a quarry to be exploited for selfish and short-range economic reasons, but as a garden to be cultivated for the development of its own potentialities of the human adventure. The goal of this relationship is not the maintenance of the status quo, but the emergence of new phenomena and new values."
René Dubos (1901–1982), bacteriologist at Rockefeller University and Pulitzer Prize recipient

The history of corporate social responsibility

An organisation* is inevitably intertwined with the society[†] in which it operates and interacts willingly or otherwise with it. It will usually make some positive contributions to society. Organisations of all types may create employment and social environments, they may provide goods, services and information needed by their customers or service users, and they generally invest in communities by paying salaries to employees and taxes to governments. But they can also have negative impacts. The downsides might include environmental damage by polluting land, the air and water, poor workforce conditions resulting in injuries, disability or illness to workers, or unreasonable exploitation of people – for example very long hours, or employing children.

CSR involves acknowledging these negative impacts and promoting ways of eliminating or mitigating them as much as possible. In this chapter we'll start by looking at the origins of CSR and consider whether it's here to stay or just the latest fashion. Is CSR a new concept? If not, where did it come from?

Depending on your definition of CSR, its origins vary, but probably date from about 4,000 years ago. What is the history of protecting and

---

* By 'organisation' we mean any sort of established or informal entity, including legally founded companies and charities, public sector organisations, partnerships and sole traders, clubs and societies, and similar groups.

[†] By 'society' we mean all organisations, governments, regulators, neighbours, individuals and media with interests in the community.

defending the rights of communities? And what records of this survive today? Another important question is what should be included in any commitment to social responsibility:

- workers' rights?
- health and safety?
- personal health and fitness?
- ethical trading?
- environmental impact?
- bribery and corrupt practices?

The earliest quoted community framework was the Hammurabi Codex, dating to 1780 BC (King, 2004). This code of law was carved on a black stone monument 2.4 metres high for public view in ancient Babylon in Mesopotamia. It included these laws:

> If a builder build a house for someone, and does not construct it properly, and the house which he built fall in and kill its owner, then that builder shall be put to death. [Law 229]
>
> If it kill the son of the owner the son of that builder shall be put to death. [Law 230]
>
> If it kill a slave of the owner, then he shall pay for a slave to the owner of the house. [Law 231]
>
> If it ruin goods, he shall make compensation for all that has been ruined, and inasmuch as he did not construct properly this house which he built and it fell, he shall re-erect the house from his own means. [Law 232]

Was this the beginning of CSR, building regulations and health and safety?

It's hard to establish for certain where CSR started. It has evolved from many disconnected disciplines. From ancient times, mankind has battled with the dilemma of making gain through the exploitation of others. Where a society has imposed some rule or regulation to encourage 'fairness', its rules have been dependent on the society's definition of equality. The Code of Hammurabi aims to protect society but also explicitly refers to slavery! Similarly, in our modern world, the approach to protecting UK workers may be different from the approach to workers overseas. And what about animals? Should we consider their suffering too?

We don't have to look as far back as ancient Mesopotamia to see the value of CSR. In the context of the British Empire, the Slave Trade Act, which outlawed trading of slaves, received Royal Assent in 1807, some five years after the earliest recognised health and safety legislation, the Health and Morals of Apprentices Act 1802. But slavery was still legal in the British overseas territories until the Slavery Abolition Act received assent in 1833. In the same year, the Factory Act established a regular working day in the textile industry, and wider protection for workers. The main provisions were that:

- children under nine could not be employed in textile factories
- children aged nine to 13 could work a maximum of nine hours per day and 48 hours per week
- young people aged 13 to 18 could work a maximum of 12 hours per day and 69 hours per week
- night work for children and young people was not permitted
- children were to attend school.

The 1833 Act also appointed four independent factory inspectors to cover the whole of the country, with the power to investigate accidents and to prosecute factory and mill owners. These principles, over 175 years old in the UK, still form part of CSR standards today, such as the Ethical Base Code for sourcing suppliers in developing nations, which, among others, includes the principles that:

- employment should be freely chosen
- working conditions should be safe and hygienic
- child labour mustn't be used
- working hours should not be excessive
- no harsh or inhumane treatment is allowed.

During the Victorian period in Britain, the development of CSR continued. Increasing industrialisation led to more pollution and a degradation of living conditions for many, affecting the health and productivity of workers. In 19th century Britain, there were no fewer than 10 Factories Acts that sought to reform working conditions. Some Victorian philanthropists realised that social reform, including relocating workers from slums to out-of-town developments, benefited not only the workers but business as well. These philanthropists' legacy lives on today in the form of businesses formed then which still survive, such as Cadbury's, Rowntree's and Lloyds Bank. However, not everyone had access to such positive opportunities.

The Victorian age saw the development of a range of piecemeal and industry-specific legislation, such as the Shop Hours Regulation Act 1886 and the Metalliferous Mines Regulation Act 1872. These were later

Job Opportunity – Child chimney sweep

Small boys between the ages of 5 and 10 are sought to clamber up chimneys. Plenty of encouragement is provided by a lighted straw held beneath your feet or by pins stuck into you.

Sweeps have other things to look forward to:

- twisted spines and kneecaps
- deformed ankles
- eye inflammations and respiratory illnesses
- 'chimney sweep's cancer', which appears in the testicles from the constant irritation of the soot on naked skin
- injuries from falls and burns
- suffocation if trapped in the curves of chimneys

consolidated into the Factory and Workshop Act 1901. This Act gave the power to the Secretary of State to make regulations for particular industries, separating Parliament from the day-to-day setting of regulations, a process which remains in place today.

This period also saw the beginnings of ecology in the era of classification and exploration of the natural world. Darwin's book *On the origin of species*, first published in 1859, led to an awakening in the scientific understanding of the natural world. This interest prompted the quest to identify and classify species, resulting in macabre but colourful collections of butterflies, beetles and birds pinned, stuffed or bottled in formaldehyde.

The early 20th century saw a new power in CSR – the tort of negligence and the principle of 'neighbour'. While the concept of 'negligence' had existed in common law for many centuries, it tended to apply only in the narrow context of a contractual 'master and servant' relationship. The famous case in 1932 of the snail in the ginger beer* extended this duty to take 'reasonable care to avoid acts or omissions which you can reasonably foresee would be likely to injure your neighbour'. This established what is known as the 'neighbour principle'.

The possibility for legal claims for compensation became a new battleground for CSR, and this continues to allow individuals, groups and communities to mount legal challenges against large organisations, with

* Donoghue *vs* Stevenson, 1932 All ER Rep 1; [1932] AC 562; House of Lords.

financial implications large enough to compel them to consider their actions in a wider context. CSR is an extension of this principle. Case law has developed to extend the neighbour principle to trespassers who you could reasonably foresee may enter your site, to contractors under your supervision, and to users of your products or services. In a globalised market place, who will be your 'neighbour' tomorrow? Could the Inuit living inside the Arctic Circle sue developed nations for the loss of the Greenland ice shelf, and thus their homes, as a result of climate change?

The increasing democracy of wealth, production and growth which followed the end of World War II took a while to gain momentum. But this also brought its problems. Thick 'pea soup' smog in London in the 1950s brought the capital to a standstill for five days, and led to the reported death of around 4,000 people from respiratory and other diseases. In response, the first Clean Air Act was introduced in 1956; it was updated in 1968 and 1993. A few years later, the publication of *Silent Spring* by Rachel Carson in 1962 questioned the impact of pesticides on the wider environment, and made society question the impact of organisations on society and the environment. This laid the foundations for the public appetite for the modern environmental movement, and for CSR.

In 1974, the UK Health and Safety at Work etc Act received Royal Assent. This new law provided 'umbrella' legislation for the protection of virtually all workers in Great Britain, and has been extended to cover offshore installations within British territorial waters. The Act has many elements that are important for the CSR practitioner.

The general duty for every employer to 'ensure so far as is reasonably practicable the health, safety and welfare at work of all his employees' brings a standardised statutory framework across industrial sectors, although there are some exclusions, such as a domestic servant in a private household. This duty implies the common approach of balancing the size of a risk against the cost of its solution, a philosophy that can be extended to CSR. The Act also sets out duties to protect 'those not in his [the employer's] employment' and places duties on designers, manufacturers, importers and suppliers which, together with consumer protection legislation (such as the Sale of Goods Act 1979), codify every organisation's legal duties to consider society, the wider public and users in its operations and interactions.

The Health and Safety at Work etc Act also requires organisations with five or more employees to have a written statement of health and safety policy. Could – and should – this be extended to include a statement of CSR and environmental protection policy for all organisations in years to come? What if every organisation had a legal duty to use the earth's resources as efficiently as is reasonably practicable?

In 1975, the CITES (Convention on International Trade in Endangered Species of Wild Fauna and Flora) list came into force. This outlawed trade in any species listed as endangered by signatory countries. While this is a voluntary code, it signalled the ability of governments to agree international protocols on environmental grounds. Today, the following are on the CITES endangered lists:

- Mammals – 679 species
- Birds – 1,475 species
- Reptiles – 676 species
- Amphibians – 114 species
- Fish – 86 species
- Invertebrates – 2,184 species
- Plants – 28,987 species.

(Source: www.cites.org/eng/disc/species.shtml)

The Ethiopian famines of the 1980s brought the inequality of where people live to every television set in the world. Scenes of wide-eyed babies, with skeletal limbs and flies around their mouths, held in the arms of a rocking mother became burned into our minds. These were famines of biblical proportions, and with millions dead from starvation and thirst, it forced millions of people in the developed world to question their own lifestyles and ask how they could help.

'Compassion fatigue' may have taken hold in later years, but the Live Aid images from 1985 opened another generation's minds to the principles of CSR and personal social responsibility (PSR), with charitable fundraising moving from the individual to the national government agenda.

While environmental and social issues had been discussed in academia for some time, they now began to reach a wider public awareness. In 1987, the Brundtland Report *Our common future* highlighted the importance of including environmental and social elements in the economic framework, and provided a widely quoted definition of sustainable development:

> Development that meets the needs of the present, without compromising the ability of future generations to meet their own needs.

One year afterwards, the Intergovernmental Panel on Climate Change (IPCC) was formed. This panel of experts and politicians was drawn from a wide range of backgrounds, including climatology and

An audience of 72,000 attended the Live Aid concert at Wembley Stadium in 1985. A further 90,000 filled the JFK Stadium in Philadelphia, while a global audience of 1.5 billion in 100 countries watched the concerts on television

oceanography. The IPCC has played a critical role in building a consensus on climate change processes, effects and adaptation strategies. It was clear that only through international agreement would any single state consider it worthwhile to introduce environmental protection at a scale that would have a reasonable effect. Several such agreements have since been signed, including the Montreal Protocol on Ozone Depleting Substances (1989) and a series of Earth Summits (most notably at Rio de Janeiro in 1992 and Kyoto in 1997) which led to 'Agenda 21' and a treaty to stabilise greenhouse gas concentrations in the atmosphere at a level that would prevent dangerous man-made influences on the climate.

Once our natural splendour is destroyed, it can never be recaptured.
Lyndon B Johnson, US President, 1963–1969

Let us remember as we chase our dreams into the stars that our first responsibility is to our Earth, to our children and to ourselves.
George H W Bush, US President, 1989–1993

Prospects for success in the world's struggle to combat global warming were transformed in November 2008 when the US President-elect, Barack Obama, made it clear that America would play its full part in renewing the Kyoto Protocol treaty on climate change. His words brought to an end eight years of objections to Kyoto by George W Bush's administration, which withdrew the US from the treaty in 2001.

President Bush had justified withdrawal from Kyoto by casting doubt on whether climate change was happening and whether it was caused by human activities. The scientific consensus on both points has become so great that the US administration had to accept that they were true.

President Obama's words have injected a new mood of optimism among negotiators preparing for the conference at which the Kyoto agreement will be renewed and extended, which is due to take place at Copenhagen in December 2009.

> Once I take office, you can be sure that the United States will once again engage vigorously in these negotiations, and help lead the world toward a new era of global co-operation on climate change.
> *Barack Obama, US President, 2009–*

This change of heart signals that the US is at last coming in from the cold – an essential prerequisite for success at Copenhagen. The conference will try to map out a way for the world to hold global temperature rises to two degrees Celsius above the pre-industrial level. This is regarded as the maximum short-term increase the earth and its human communities can safely sustain.

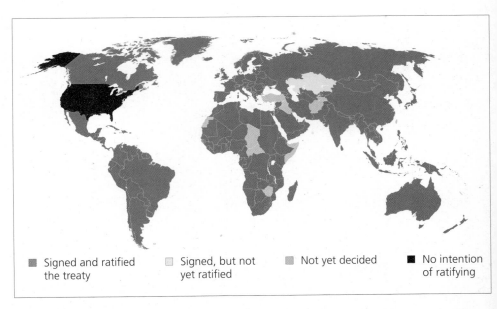

Map showing the 178 states (at April 2008) which have ratified the Kyoto Protocol to the United Nations Framework Convention on Climate Change

■ Signed and ratified the treaty   □ Signed, but not yet ratified   ■ Not yet decided   ■ No intention of ratifying

The signatories to the Kyoto Protocol have agreed to limit greenhouse gas emissions. While some countries have reduction targets, developing countries must control their increases. The European Union agreed to an 8 per cent reduction in carbon dioxide equivalent emissions, based on 1990 emission levels, by 2012. These reduction agreements expire in 2013, when a new agreement will be needed.

The Kyoto agreement set in motion the legal framework that has resulted in an EU-wide carbon emissions trading scheme and the UK climate change regulatory framework, which creates:

> [a] new approach to managing and responding to climate change in the UK through setting ambitious targets, taking powers to help achieve them, strengthening the institutional framework, enhancing the UK's ability to adapt to the impact of climate change and establishing clear and regular accountability to the UK Parliament.
> *Department for the Environment, Food and Rural Affairs*

This new target-setting approach is likely to lead to increasing pressure on UK organisations to report and minimise their greenhouse gas emissions. Performance so far in a selection of countries against their agreed obligations is shown below.

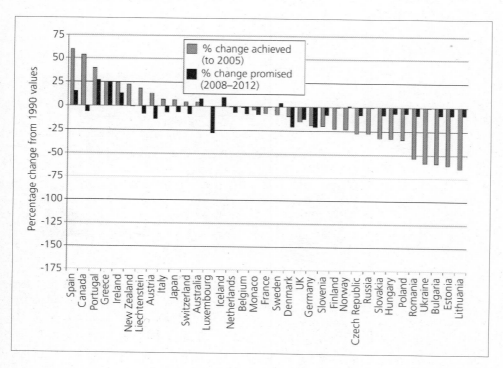

Changes in greenhouse gas emissions by Kyoto signatory countries since 1990

CSR's dramatic evolution over the last generation hasn't been limited to the environmental risk area. Other risk areas, such as bribery and corruption, fair trade and ethical sourcing, are all now central to the core principles of what CSR is or should be. In January 1999, the UN Secretary-General Kofi Annan challenged world business leaders to embrace and enact the United Nations Global Compact. This agreement seeks support for nine principles of human rights, labour and environmental sustainability as they apply to business practices and public policy. The past decade has seen the development of recognised auditable standards such as ISO 14001 (for environmental management), SA 8000 (for social accountability) and ISO 26000 (for CSR) to allow third parties to distinguish between the truth and the hype of organisations' CSR claims. The standards are summarised in Chapter 6.

These standards include the principles of international human rights norms as described in International Labour Organization conventions, the United Nations Convention on the Rights of the Child, and the Universal Declaration of Human Rights. The last focuses on:

- child labour
- forced labour
- health and safety
- free association
- collective bargaining
- discrimination
- disciplinary practices
- working hours
- compensation.

Ethics *vs* the need to compete in the global economy

As we've already discussed, organisations inevitably interact with the societies and macro-environments within which they operate. In this book, you'll learn the key points in relation to CSR (and, in Chapter 9, PSR) and how some organisations are working to tackle these issues.

We'll look at the benefits for organisations and society which can be gained from broad adoption of CSR principles, and also the potential difficulties of trying to balance ethical practice against the need to compete in a global economy.

We've already shown that organisations can have both positive and negative impacts on society. Without organisations, we'd have no goods or services, no employment, and reduced tax revenues to fund the public sector in areas such as health, education and welfare support. But with the increasing commercialisation and globalisation of business, there are potential negative impacts too.

Fundamentally, businesses operate to make profits and to grow year on year. Other organisations will have other objectives, for example to provide information or charity. Businesses are often seen as the 'bad guys'. Their need to expand and make profits for their owners or shareholders can sometimes be to the detriment of society and the environment. This presents businesses and society with a dilemma: how to balance the needs of society against the benefits of a dynamic and developing economy.

Test your thinking 1

To bring these dilemmas into sharp focus, consider the following scenarios:

1. If a manufacturing company chooses to move its production plant from the UK to the Far East to reduce costs, what impact will this have on the local economy and local suppliers? If it does not move, it might be undercut by a competitor and close.

2. What are the effects if a furniture supplier has a sustainable purchasing policy? Its decision not to sell tropical hardwoods from rainforests may mean it has to increase the price to its customers of the goods it sells.

3. How much money should an oil company invest in leak detection systems in pipelines when it extracts oil in sensitive tundra or marine environments, such as Alaska?

4. If a company invests significant resources to extract minerals in an underdeveloped country, how should subsequent profits be divided between the local community, the country's government and the investors who funded the work?

All of these examples represent real issues to businesses and governments across the world. Companies, governments and people have to engage with each other to make sure that the net benefit of business is to society, and not just to a few individuals.

Test your thinking 2

Let's take the UK supermarket sector as an example. Since the 1980s, there has been a significant increase in the number of big supermarkets in the UK. These supermarkets are generally controlled by four big chains – Tesco, Asda/Walmart, Sainsbury's and Morrison's. As these chains have expanded, smaller retailers have struggled to compete as the market leaders have significant advantages in terms of buying power and stock availability.

The large supermarkets provide quick access to a wide choice of goods at low prices, but this can come at a cost, causing damage to local communities, local economies and the environment. The big supermarket chains can now wield a huge influence over our lives – economically, socially, environmentally and culturally. Suppose a new supermarket is being built in your area. What positive and negative impacts would the new facility bring? The extract below outlines some of the positive impacts claimed for a new supermarket.

> Independent planning consultants looked at our new store in Beverley....
> Far from damaging Beverley and its economy, the study found that Tesco acted as a magnet.... Two-thirds of our customers visit other stores in the town centre, and local business leaders say that it has boosted Beverley's reputation as a place where people want to go to shop. So I would argue that strong supermarkets can also benefit local economies and local people.
> *Sir Terry Leahy, chief executive officer of Tesco, at the IGD Conference, October 2004*

The quotation below outlines some of the negative impacts of a new supermarket.

> East Riding Council says we must have a Tesco ... because footfall will bring trade into the town centre. But Tesco has caused a loss of distinctiveness, a change in the texture of the town. Take a look at what is on offer in Tesco compared to the home-baked pies and cakes in the deli. I can't imagine the discerning visitors we say we want to attract will keep on coming when they realise what is happening. Beverley's charm is declining and its prosperity has very little to do with multinationals, pound shops and mobile phone outlets.
> *Retired lecturer and Beverley resident, Richard Wilson*

The following questions should help you to explore the CSR-related impacts in this scenario fully.

1. Make a list of some other positive impacts of the new supermarket.

2. Make a list of some other negative impacts of the new supermarket.

Here are some suggested answers to help you develop your understanding.

The positive impacts could include:

- employment
- local investment
- additional facilities
- better accessibility
- redevelopment of disused land or buildings
- re-investment
- local supply chain development
- increased choice for consumers
- lower prices
- increased local business
- improved infrastructure and roads
- relocated public services.

The negative impacts could include:

- impact on local businesses, eg loss of trade
- habitat destruction
- increased traffic
- less accessibility if an out-of-town development
- loss of community
- use of resources
- litter
- noise
- waste
- 'ghost town' effect
- loss of distinctiveness
- the 'clone town' effect (all towns the same)
- loss of essential services such as post offices, car parks and access to public transport
- loss of public and community space.

Depending on the location of the supermarket and the surrounding conditions, the balance of the negative and positive impacts could result in a net benefit or net loss to the community. If organisations don't consider and consult communities, planning permission may not be granted for the new development or customers could boycott their stores or products. In this information and media age, pressure groups can be formed and information easily distributed to highlight the impacts that organisations have.

CSR – what does it mean?

We've seen that the decisions that companies make can have a dramatic effect on society, economics and the environment. CSR really is all about organisations acknowledging their interactions with the environment and society, and considering and responding to the implications of the decisions they make.

Different organisations have different definitions of CSR, although there's considerable common ground between them. Consider the following definitions:

> Corporate Social Responsibility is the continuing commitment by business to behave ethically and contribute to economic development while improving the quality of life of the workforce and their families as well as of the local community and society at large.
> Richard Holme and Phil Watts in Making good business sense (World Business Council for Sustainable Development 2000)

Or there's this slimmed down version from the Philippines:

> CSR is about business giving back to society.

The UK Chartered Institute of Public Relations defines CSR as:

> ... a concept whereby companies integrate social and environmental concerns in their business operations and in their interaction with their stakeholders on a voluntary basis.

The UK government sees CSR as:

> ... the business contribution to our sustainable development goals. Essentially it is about how business takes account of its economic, social and environmental impacts in the way it operates – maximising the benefits and minimising the downsides. Specifically, we see CSR as the voluntary actions that business can take, over and above compliance with minimum legal requirements, to address both its own competitive interests and the interests of wider society.
> UK government CSR website, www.csr.gov.uk

The UK Business Impact Task Force says:

> Corporate Social Responsibility, addressed comprehensively, can deliver the greatest benefits to a company and its stakeholders when integrated with business strategy and operations.

Test your thinking 3
Considering these examples, how would you define CSR in your own words?

Chapter 3: The appetite for CSR

"When your house is worthless, food costs more than gold, you are facing redundancy and petrol is a million pounds a gallon, you are hardly likely to spend a hundred quid on some shrivelled up [organic] mushroom just so a polar bear can have a bigger playground."
Jeremy Clarkson, BBC TV presenter, 'Top Gear'

"It is important to save the Earth, because that's all we have. We don't get another."
Amy Larrick, aged nine, of Rockford, Illinois (from a display at EPCOT Park, Florida)

Brands, media and CSR

Current business norms show a persistent and growing use of branding and logos in advertising as part of concerted communication and marketing campaigns. As consumers become increasingly aware of their social responsibilities, organisations seek to meet their needs by providing real or perceived 'green' and 'friendly' products.

A major criticism of CSR is that organisations may care more about their brand than the people it might affect – that it's more about media, marketing and presentation than actually making a real difference.

> Not whitewash, but greenwash!
> *Anon.*

For many organisations, their brands are likely to be some of their core assets – some organisations go as far as to put a monetary value on their brands in their accounts. This is as true of the large multinational companies as of the pressure groups that seek to influence them.

Test your thinking 4

Think of some well-known organisations and their brands – the biggest, strongest brands you've heard of. Below are the names of some example organisations. What does their brand make you think of?

- Body Shop
- World Wide Fund for Nature
- McDonald's
- Greenpeace
- Adidas

We've prepared some possible responses, based on common views of these organisations. Compare them with your own.

1. Body Shop – an ethically based chain established by the late Anita Roddick, which has recently been bought by a large pharmaceutical company. It sells a range of plant-based cosmetics, body scrubs and lotions. Avoids animal testing.

2. The World Wide Fund for Nature – an environmental charity that campaigns to save species at risk of extinction, such as pandas, polar bears and tigers.

3. McDonald's – a place to get cheap fast food, but we wonder how good it is for us. Happy Meals include collectible toys for children. Starting to add salads to menus.

4. Greenpeace – an environmental pressure group that believes in direct action to get media publicity. Some members occupied the Brent Spar oil platform in the North Sea a few years ago. Their ship, called *Rainbow Warrior*, was sunk in New Zealand.

5. Adidas – a leading sportswear brand worn by top athletes. Three stripes. German. Often faked.

Organisations spend large quantities of money to create a brand image and protect it. As we become more aware of CSR, we may start to think that organisations should include some of the CSR-related issues within their branding. Whether the brand is based on ethical trading, such as the Body Shop, or whether it's a fast food retailer or even a tobacco company, 'image' is critical if it's to remain profitable and viable in the longer term.

Naomi Klein provides a fascinating review of branding in her book *No Logo*, which became one of the most influential texts about the anti-globalisation movement, and an international bestseller. Throughout the book's four parts – No Space, No Choice, No Jobs and No Logo – the author comments on issues such as sweatshops, culture-jamming and corporate censorship. She pays special attention to the deeds and misdeeds of some of the organisations we asked you to consider earlier.

In this media age, the internet allows anyone to publish virtually anything without any sort of proof or validation. It can be difficult to establish what to believe and what not to.

Test your thinking 5

Here are two articles about the Body Shop – one from a pressure group and one from the organisation itself.

Fuelling consumption at the Earth's expense

Body Shop has over 1,500 stores in 47 countries, and aggressive expansion plans. Their main purpose (like many multinationals) is making lots of money for their rich shareholders. In other words, they are driven by power and greed. But the Body Shop try to conceal this reality by continually pushing the message that by shopping at their stores, rather than elsewhere, people will help solve some of the world's problems. The truth is that nobody can make the world a better place by shopping.

Natural products?

Body Shop gives the impression that their products are made from mostly natural ingredients. In fact, like all big cosmetic companies, they make wide use of non-renewable petrochemicals, synthetic colours, fragrances and preservatives, and in many of their products they use only tiny amounts of botanical-based ingredients.

Body Shop claims to be helping some third world workers and indigenous peoples through so-called 'Trade Not Aid' or 'Community Trade' projects. In fact, these are largely a marketing ploy as less than 1 per cent of sales go to 'Community Trade' producers.
Source: www.mcspotlight.org

1. Does this article make you reconsider your image of the Body Shop? If so, how?

2. How far do you think a company such as this that sells consumer products should go in marketing a green image?

Now read the Body Shop's statement:

We take our commitment to ethical trade seriously and our approach is one of constructive engagement and capacity building. We believe that we should source from suppliers who share our values and support them in providing ethical employment standards. But what do we do when a supplier just won't co-operate?

In 2004, we conducted 62 on-site factory audits and worked successfully with suppliers around the world to improve the working conditions of their employees. However, in the course of the year, Body Shop also had to disengage from five suppliers – located in China, the Philippines and

Taiwan – as a result of their failure to meet our ethical standards. The decision to disengage from each of these suppliers was based on their lack of commitment to improving working standards.

For example, in the case of a factory in China, an audit identified that the supplier was not paying medical insurance for workers. We offered to contribute towards the cost of medical insurance, but the supplier refused to participate on the basis that the Body Shop business made up only a small part of their total sales. Due to this non-compliance we withdrew our orders from this supplier.
Body Shop 'Values' report, 2005

1. How far do you think a company should go in managing the impacts of its suppliers?

2. Which do you believe more – the first (from the pressure group) or the second (from Body Shop)? Why?

3. Does the Body Shop's own statement give them more credibility?

4. What are the dangers of only reading one source of information about a company's performance on CSR?

As we've seen, it's important to look and read very carefully – to look beyond the 'greenwash' and to do our homework – if we're truly to fulfil our appetites for CSR.

The only way of finding the limits of the possible is by going beyond them into the impossible.
Arthur C Clarke (1917–2008)

Nature never did betray the heart that loved her.
William Wordsworth (1770–1850)

Chapter 4: Stakeholder expectations

"A Corporation [is] an ingenious device for obtaining individual profit without individual responsibility."
Ambrose Bierce (1842–1914)

Society

A society is a diverse but connected population of humans interacting in an economic, social and industrial infrastructure. What impact is your organisation having on society?

A central principle of CSR focuses on how an organisation relates to all of its stakeholders. The CSR concept is that we should look at the impacts of our organisation 'beyond the factory gates'. As we saw in Chapter 2, throughout the evolution of CSR, the standards to which an organisation should operate have varied according to its location in both time and place. The society in which the organisation operates will have a range of expectations, but in the global village – full of conflicting agendas and pressures – how can any organisation hope to measure up to the expectations of everyone else?

In this chapter, we'll look at some of the pressures stakeholders can bring to bear on organisations, and the approaches that can be used to manage these expectations in an increasingly media-led age.

Stakeholders

Society is increasingly interested in the impact of organisations' activities. Society, and its media and special interest groups, looks at what organisations have done – good or bad – in terms of their products and services, their impact on the environment and local communities, and how they treat and develop their workforces.

While the precise definition may vary, the groups of people interested or affected by the organisation's activities are called 'stakeholders'. One definition of 'stakeholders' is provided by the International Finance Corporation, part of the World Bank:

> Stakeholders are persons or groups who are directly or indirectly affected by a project, as well as those who may have interests in a project and/or the ability to influence its outcome, either positively or negatively. Stakeholders may include locally affected communities or individuals and their formal and informal representatives, national or local government authorities, politicians, religious leaders, civil society organizations and

groups with special interests, the academic community, or other businesses.

Source: Stakeholder engagement: a good practice handbook for companies doing business in emerging markets *(2007)*

The stakeholders of an organisation may include:

- customers (consumers of our products or services)
- employees (on our payroll)
- suppliers and contractors (the people we do business with)
- shareholders (who provided the money for the enterprise and expect to be rewarded)
- society (everyone else, including government, regulators, media and the public).

We want you to understand who the specific stakeholders may be in a particular organisation. One way to do this is to develop a 'mind map'. Mind mapping is a useful tool to help you think about complex ideas and issues, and find connectivity between themes. To make notes on a subject using a mind map, make a sketch in the following way:

- write the title of the subject in the centre of the page, and draw a circle around it
- for the major subject subheadings, draw lines out from this circle; label these lines with the subheadings
- if you have another tier of information belonging to the subheadings, draw these and link them to the subheading lines
- finally, for individual facts or ideas, draw lines out from the appropriate heading line and label them
- as you come across new information, link it in to the mind map appropriately.

For more information on the mind mapping approach, visit www.mindtools.com/pages/article/newISS_01.htm.

Test your thinking 6
Choose a major sports equipment manufacturer and develop a mind map to identify as many of its stakeholders as possible.

Include, for example, customers, employees, shareholders, media, pressure groups and governments – what will their key objectives be and what kind of pressure could they apply?

The typical stakeholders of a sports equipment manufacturer could include:

- customers – eg retail outlets
- consumers – end users
- suppliers
- retail traders
- sports governing bodies
- athletes and sporting participants
- endorsing personalities
- endorsing teams
- employees
- neighbours
- governments
- non-governmental organisations
- health advisers
- media companies (including those that sell advertising space)
- pressure groups
- investors or shareholders
- insurance companies.

Each stakeholder will doubtless have their own opinions, motivations and interests, which can quite easily come into conflict with each other. Crucially, each stakeholder will exert different types and levels of pressure.

Test your thinking 7

Below is a list of the sports equipment manufacturer's six main stakeholder groups. Think about what each group's key objectives are and how they could apply pressure to the company to get what they want.

- customers
- employees
- shareholders
- the media
- pressure groups
- the government.

The following table gives some examples of what the stakeholders may want and how they could achieve it.

Group	Objectives	Means of applying pressure
Customers	Good quality, stylish products at a reasonable price	Buying other products if they are better
Employees	Good pay and conditions, safe working environment, long-term secure employment	Internal requests, strikes, contact with media
Shareholders	Return on their investment through share dividends, profits and capital growth in the shares	Direct shareholder pressure on management or by investing in alternative businesses
Media	To increase their revenue through greater circulation and more advertising	Interesting (negative?) news stories of interest to the wider public
Pressure groups	To further the cause of the group	Direct action, bad publicity, alternative reports. Providing information to other groups such as shareholders or consumers
Government	Protect society, maintain votes	Information, policy, tax incentives and regulation

The figure on the opposite page illustrates some of the competitive forces found in the business environment.

Now consider your own organisation. Who are its stakeholders? How could they apply pressure? How could you manage these relationships?

Stakeholder engagement

The function of managing the relationships and expectations of the people and groups your organisation is likely to affect is called 'stakeholder engagement'. The aim of stakeholder engagement is not to gain unanimous consensus, for this would probably be impossible. It includes consulting proactively with key stakeholders in order to decide how best to manage your organisation's CSR-related impacts – in other words, in a way that mitigates negative impacts and maximises the contribution of positive impacts. The key principles of effective engagement include:

- providing meaningful information in a format and language that is readily understandable and tailored to meet the needs of the target stakeholder group

The business in society
*Source: www.
mallenbaker.net*

- providing information in advance of consultation activities and decision-making
- sharing information in ways and locations that make it easy for stakeholders to access it
- respect for local traditions, languages, timeframes, and decision-making processes
- two-way dialogue that gives both sides the opportunity to exchange views and information, to listen and to have their issues heard and addressed (such as open meetings)
- making sure that the views of traditionally disadvantaged groups are heard equally
- processes that are free of intimidation or coercion
- clear mechanisms for responding to people's concerns, suggestions and grievances
- incorporating feedback into the proposed project or programme design, and reporting back to stakeholders.

The depth, style, nature and frequency of this engagement with key stakeholders depends on a range of factors, including:

- the nature and scale of the activity – the more impact the organisation is likely to have on society and the environment, the greater the level of engagement needed
- the stage of the project – new installations or shutdowns are likely to alter the status of the organisation or affect its stakeholders. Change is likely to raise more concern than continuing with the status quo
- statutory requirements – depending on the type, scale and impact on the environment or working conditions, the law may require the organisation to engage its stakeholders
- the target group – its characteristics and how easy it is to engage with
- resource availability – how much time, labour and money the organisation has available to invest in an engagement programme
- economic sector – public sector initiatives are likely to require more in-depth engagement than private sector projects
- location – the local environment may be especially sensitive (eg it's close to a Site of Special Scientific Interest), or the project may be close to a school, hospital, place of worship or residential area
- organisational policy – what the organisation's long term approach is for engaging with its key stakeholders.

The different levels of stakeholder engagement can vary from simple information provision as part of a drive to be more transparent through to in-depth negotiations, where the extended involvement leads to participants materially contributing to the formulation of proposals and the organisation's operations.

Stakeholder engagement can be broken down into eight key areas, as defined by Mallen Baker:

- Stakeholder identification and analysis. Invest time in identifying and prioritising stakeholders and assessing their interests and concerns.
- Information disclosure. Communicate information to stakeholders early in the decision-making process, in ways that are meaningful and accessible, and continue this communication throughout the project.
- Stakeholder consultation. Plan out each consultation process, consult inclusively, document the process and communicate subsequent decisions.
- Negotiation and partnerships. For controversial and complex issues, negotiate in good faith in a way that satisfies the interests of all parties. Add value to the project's benefits and your plans to mitigate impacts by forming strategic partnerships.

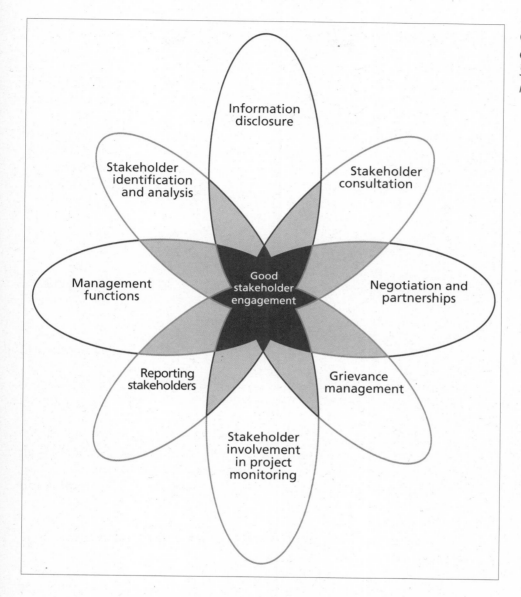

Good stakeholder engagement
Source: www. mallenbaker.net

- Grievance management. Establish accessible and responsive means for stakeholders to raise concerns and grievances about the project throughout its life.
- Stakeholder involvement in project monitoring. Involve stakeholders in monitoring project impacts, mitigation and benefits, and involve external monitors where they can improve transparency and credibility.
- Reporting to stakeholders. Report back to stakeholders on environmental, social and economic performance. Include stakeholders that you've consulted directly and those with more general interests in the project and parent company.

- Management functions. Build and maintain sufficient capacity within the organisation to manage processes of stakeholder engagement, track commitments, and report on progress.

The figure on the previous page outlines the key elements of these core areas.

The core principles can be developed into a detailed stakeholder engagement plan, which sets out a clear standard for your organisation's approach to working with its key stakeholders.

Stakeholder engagement plan

A good stakeholder engagement plan should:

- describe requirements for consultation and disclosure imposed by regulators, lenders, the organisation itself and others
- identify the key stakeholder groups and prioritise work with them
- provide a strategy and timetable for sharing information and consulting with each of these groups
- describe resources and responsibilities for implementing stakeholder engagement activities
- explain how stakeholder engagement activities will be incorporated into the organisation's management system.

The scope and level of detail of the plan should be scaled to fit the needs of the project or operation. This example, based on guidelines from the World Bank Group in *Stakeholder engagement: a good practice handbook for companies doing business in emerging markets*, follows the process through in 10 logical sections.

1. Introduction

Brief description of the project (or the organisation's operations), including design elements and potential social and environmental issues. Where relevant, include maps of the project site and surrounding area.

2. Regulations and requirements

Summarise the legal, regulatory, lender or organisational requirements for stakeholder engagement that are relevant to the project or the organisation's operations. This may involve a requirement for public consultation and disclosure during the social and environmental assessment process.

3. Summary of any previous stakeholder engagement activities

If your organisation has already carried out any activities, including information disclosure and consultation, add the following details:

- the type of information disclosed and in what forms (eg presentations, brochure, reports, posters, radio)
- the locations and dates of any meetings held so far
- individuals, groups and organisations that have been consulted
- key issues that have been discussed and key concerns raised
- agreements that have been reached
- the organisation's response to issues raised, including any commitments or follow-up actions
- the process chosen for documenting these activities and reporting back to stakeholders.

4. Project or organisational stakeholders

List the key stakeholder groups you'll need to tell and consult about the project or operations. These should include people or groups that:

- are directly or indirectly affected by the project (or the organisation's operations)
- have commercial or financial interests in the project or organisation
- have the potential to influence project outcomes or operations, such as affected communities, neighbour organisations, NGOs and government authorities. Stakeholders can also include individual politicians, other organisations, trade unions, academics, religious groups, national social and environmental public sector agencies, and the media.

5. Stakeholder engagement programme

Summarise the purpose and goals of the programme (either project-specific or corporate), and describe what information will be disclosed and in what formats, and the types of method that will be used to communicate this information to each of the stakeholder groups identified. The methods you use may vary according to the target audience, for example:

- newspapers, posters, radio, television and the internet
- information centres and exhibitions or other visual displays
- brochures, leaflets, non-technical summary documents and reports
- interviews with stakeholder representatives
- surveys, polls and questionnaires
- public meetings, workshops and focus groups
- participatory methods – encouraging people to become lay members of working groups and management teams
- other traditional mechanisms for consultation and decision-making, such as involving local councils.

6. Timetable

Draw up a schedule which outlines the dates and locations of stakeholder engagement activities.

7. Resources and responsibilities

List the staff and resources which will be allocated to managing and implementing the organisation's stakeholder engagement programme. Add details of:

- who within the organisation will be responsible for carrying out these activities
- what budget has been allocated toward these activities.

For projects or complex operations with significant or diverse impacts and multiple stakeholder groups, it's good practice to recruit a qualified community liaison officer to arrange and facilitate these activities. Integration of the community liaison function with other core business functions is also important, as is management involvement and oversight.

8. Grievance mechanism

Describe the process by which people affected by the project or operations can bring their grievances to the organisation for consideration and redress. Describe how responses will be fed back to the correspondent.

9. Monitoring and reporting

Describe plans to involve the key stakeholders in monitoring the impacts of the project and ways of controlling them. Say how and when the results of stakeholder engagement activities will be reported back to affected stakeholders as well as broader stakeholder groups. Tools which can be used for this include:

- social and environmental assessment reports
- organisation newsletters
- annual monitoring reports
- company annual reports
- corporate sustainability reports.

10. Management functions

This section shows how stakeholder engagement activities will be integrated into the organisation's core business functions. It may include:

- the name of the management representative responsible for overseeing the programme

- the plans for hiring, training and deploying staff to undertake stakeholder engagement work
- the reporting lines between community liaison staff and senior management
- internal communication of the stakeholder engagement strategy
- the management tools which will be used to document, track and manage the process, eg a stakeholder database or commitments register (a formal record of the agreements made with stakeholders)
- details of the interaction between appointed contractors, stakeholders and the organisation.

CSR tries to manage the impact of the organisation on others and the environment. Stakeholders are the individuals and groups with which your organisation interacts – with their consent or otherwise. It's clear that you won't please every group or every individual all of the time. But through transparent disclosure of information, active engagement at relevant stages, and timely and accurate consultation, problems can be managed at the earliest stages to prevent, minimise and mitigate the possible social, economic and environmental effects not only of your organisation on your stakeholders, but also of stakeholders on your organisation.

Better the devil you know...
Kylie Minogue, Australian singer and entertainer

Chapter 5: Benefits for organisations

"To be a success in business be daring, be first, be different."
Henry Marchant (1741–1796)

Each member of an individual stakeholder group (customers, employees, suppliers, shareholders and society) can – and does – apply a range of pressures on an organisation. These pressures can also be regarded as an opportunity. By consulting wisely with these stakeholder groups, organisations can plan in detail how they're going to meet the needs and concerns of these people and groups. Doing this for all groups simultaneously can be a challenge – for example, suppliers may want to deliver more frequently to reduce their warehouse stocks, while society prefers to see fewer vehicles on the roads. But by including CSR in business planning, organisations can reap benefits, including:

- a more motivated and loyal workforce
- greater productivity
- reduced overheads and greater efficiency
- more sales
- greater access to capital
- increased customer loyalty
- improved reputation
- reduced risk of prosecution
- access to investment and larger market shares.

The following comes from a report called *Winning with integrity*, based on a survey by MORI in 2000.

Good for society, good for business

Companies which take CSR seriously not only achieve benefits to society; they can also enhance their reputation, improve competitiveness and strengthen their risk management.

Some facts and figures about CSR:

- 81 per cent of customers agree that when price and quality are equal they are more likely to buy products associated with a good cause
- 73 per cent of people agreed that they would be more loyal to an employer that supports the local community
- a recent poll indicated that 17 per cent of consumers were likely to be influenced by ethical considerations when making purchasing decisions.

An increasing number of companies of all sizes are finding that there are real business benefits from being socially responsible, as this figure shows. CSR has become a core issue for many large businesses. More than 80 per cent of FTSE-100 companies now provide information about their environmental performance, social impact or both.

Added value from CSR

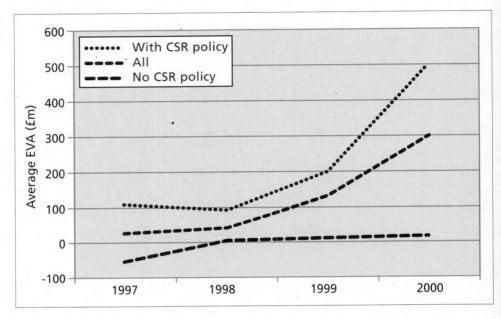

These trends are not confined to big business; a recent MORI survey of small and medium-sized enterprises found that 61 per cent were involved 'a great deal' or a 'fair amount' in the local community.*

Test your thinking 8

Consider each of the following stakeholder groups for your organisation and list the potential benefits to the organisation of a CSR policy:

- customers
- employees
- suppliers
- shareholders
- society.

* Source: Business in the Community, www.bitc.org.uk.

The scope of CSR

If an organisation is to harness these benefits, it needs to consider a wide range of factors. These include community, environment, ethics, human rights, responsibility in the market and its workforce.* Each of these factors is summarised below, before we analyse them more deeply afterwards.

Community

An organisation should consider its impacts on the local and wider community. Investment into the community may take the form of jobs and salaries, charitable donations, staff time and skills, and donations in kind. Transport is an important factor – for example, employees commuting to and from work will affect the local roads.

Environment

An organisation should identify the impact its goods and services have on the environment. As part of its planning, it should seek to minimise negative impacts, for example by investing in habitat creation schemes.

Ethics

An organisation will inevitably be judged on how it makes its decisions, and how these decisions are implemented. For example, would it be ethical to explore for fossil fuels in Antarctica, even if it were allowed?

Ethical principles reflect the values of the organisation, which are seen in the context of the values of its stakeholders and the society in which it operates.

Human rights

A civilised society recognises the right of every individual to liberty, freedom of association, free speech and personal safety. These form the basis for codes of human rights found at the core of national and international laws, such as the UN Declaration of Human Rights.

Responsibility in the market

Organisations can have a real impact on society through their marketing activities. For example, should cigarettes or sugary drinks be advertised during screenings of films for children? Responsibility in the marketplace can strengthen organisations' competitive edge – or damage it.

---

* The principles identified here are based on those in the Business in the Community CSR toolkit.

The key issues include ethical advertising, relationships with suppliers, relationships with customers, distribution, packaging and the process of creating the product or service itself.

Workforce

Recognising organisations' impact in the workplace means understanding the business benefits and the wider social impact of good employment policies. This not only covers the traditional areas of recruitment, remuneration, training and health and safety, but also the growing concerns – and opportunities – of issues such as diversity and equal opportunities.

We will now consider each of these elements in greater detail.

Community

No organisation operates in a social vacuum. They employ people, use suppliers and have relationships with customers. Organisations' decisions on their location affect the local community, as do the employment and procurement decisions they make.

In Chapter 2 we considered the potential impacts of the location of a supermarket, but communities can be equally affected by establishing a new major manufacturing plant or closing down a mine, using local suppliers or investing in deprived areas.

By aligning the organisation's goals with the community's needs, both can benefit. A technique that's gaining increasing interest, particularly in connection with new projects, is the ESIA, or environmental and social impact assessment.

The main steps in an ESIA are:

- baseline study
- impact assessment
- management planning
- monitoring
- community consultation.

Baseline study

Field studies are carried out to assess the local demographics (including social groups), flora, fauna, water, soil and pollution levels.

Impact assessment

All the social and environmental impacts associated with a project are identified and evaluated.

Management planning

The measures aimed at avoiding, minimising and correcting the negative impacts are detailed in a management plan. There is a typical mitigation hierarchy included in management plans:

- prevent
- minimise
- restore
- compensate or offset.

Consultation and local development actions should take place throughout the process.

Monitoring

A programme of monitoring is developed and implemented to make sure that all management measures are being correctly and effectively applied.

Community consultation

Throughout all steps in this process, contact is maintained with interested parties. The most popular community initiatives tend to be links with education and charities, but joint projects are also becoming more common with local regeneration and arts organisations. By investing in local education, for example in projects such as work experience, organisations can help to develop a future workforce that meets their needs. Organisations can also consider the impact on the community of the decisions they make. They can improve 'social capital' through donations to charities or supporting voluntary organisations. In this way, organisations are perceived to be profiting with the community rather than from it.

Environment

The environment is now a critical consideration for most types of organisation whether through the money it spends on dealing with its waste, its use of energy or how and from where it buys its raw materials. Each of these factors directly affects the impact the organisation has on the environment. If an organisation can use less material and energy and create less waste, not only will it help the environment, but it'll save the company money, which, if safeguarded, goes straight to the bottom line. Early projects proving this included the Aire and Calder Project and Project Catalyst. These projects were both based on 'waste clubs', where members would meet regularly to discuss savings and how they had made them. These types of project have since been repeated by many organisations, in some cases facilitated by local authorities under the Agenda 21 banner established by the Intergovernmental Conference on Climate Change in Rio de Janeiro in 1992.

When considering the environment, organisations need to look at their functions in a structured way to identify the inputs to the organisation, the processes, and the outputs. At each stage, environmental improvement opportunities can often be identified.

Inputs
Only buy what you need, from sustainably managed resources. Avoid having to throw material away by not buying too many short-shelf-life products.

Processes
Make the most out of what you have. Use energy efficiently, turn lights and machinery off when they're not being used. Turn off computers, printers and photocopiers overnight, and don't leave electrical equipment in standby mode.

Outputs
Only dispose of what you really have to. Consider and apply the waste hierarchy – reduce, re-use and recycle before resorting to disposal. If you incorporate meaningful environmental objectives into the organisation, you'll see benefits through better use of resources, a reduction in waste, and the chance to make environmental sustainability one of your unique selling points.

The whole approach minimises your current and future environmental liabilities and reduces your corporate risk, while enhancing your business reputation.

Ethics
Every organisation relies on human relationships; they're at the heart of the interactions between the organisation and its workers, its consumers and its suppliers. By establishing clear values and principles for the organisation, each decision made throughout the enterprise can be aligned with its strategic purpose.

For any organisation to grow and develop, it needs to put long-term relationships before short-term profit. It should demonstrate its ethical principles in every way it can – for example, in the way it recruits and employs staff, in the products it offers the customer, and in the contracts it offers to its suppliers.

An ethical approach to business can be critical to the organisation's long-term success.

Human rights

If organisations are to be socially responsible, they need to take on board one of the most basic elements – a respect for human rights. The three most important internationally recognised human rights instruments are:

- the UN Universal Declaration of Human Rights
- the International Covenant of Civil and Political Rights
- the International Covenant on Economic, Social and Cultural Rights.

Together, these protocols form the International Bill of Human Rights and include a set of freedoms for every human being, regardless of race, religion or sex. These are enforced by national governments, the UN Human Rights Council and the UN Security Council, although the last was criticised for not acting in Rwanda, Bosnia and Darfur.

Test your thinking 9
What do you consider to be your basic human rights?

As a guide to answering this, it's worth looking at the International Bill of Human Rights, which includes the following rights:

- everyone has the right to life, liberty and personal security
- no-one may be held in slavery or servitude; slavery and the slave trade are prohibited in all their forms
- no-one may be subjected to torture or to cruel, inhuman or degrading treatment or punishment
- no-one may be subjected to arbitrary arrest, detention or exile
- everyone charged with a criminal offence has the right to be presumed innocent until proven guilty
- no-one's privacy may be arbitrarily interfered with
- everyone has the right to leave any country, including their own, and to return to that country
- men and women of full age, without any limitation due to race, nationality or religion, have the right to marry and to found a family
- everyone has the right to own property alone as well as in association with others
- everyone has the right to freedom of thought, conscience and religion
- everyone has the right to freedom of opinion and expression
- everyone has the right to freedom of peaceful assembly and association
- everyone has the right to take part in the government of their country, directly or through freely chosen representatives

- everyone has the right to work, to free choice of employment, to just and favourable conditions of work and to protection against unemployment
- everyone, without any discrimination, has the right to equal pay for equal work
- everyone has the right to a standard of living adequate for the health and wellbeing of themselves and their family
- everyone has the right to education.

We recommend you look at the full UN Declaration of Human Rights, available at www.hrweb.org/legal/udhr.html.

As significant players in society, organisations should check carefully that they comply with these basic human rights. Beyond this, they should consider the impact of investing in countries which don't have the same respect for human rights as their own.

Market responsibility

An organisation's impact on society in the marketplace is made up of the effect of what it produces, and how it buys and sells. How much value or harm do its products and services generate? Is its approach to marketing, advertising and procurement fair and honest, as well as effective?

While price, quality and service all play an important role in consumers' purchasing decisions, they're increasingly influenced by CSR factors, as we discussed earlier. Some consumers are now willing to pay a higher price for fair trade, ethically produced, organic or environmentally friendly products.

Test your thinking 10

1. Consider your own purchasing decisions. Would you consider, or have you considered, the impacts of what you're buying?

2. Would you boycott a company's goods on a particular issue?

3. Do you buy goods because the product is organic, not tested on animals, includes the fair trade logo? Do you avoid products from companies that have received negative publicity in the media?

4. What CSR factors influence your purchasing decisions?

Organisations are aware of their customers' answers to these questions and respond in a range of ways. Some market their products and services specifically on CSR factors – remember the Body Shop example earlier, and how it emphasises the responsible manufacture and testing of its products.

It's important to recognise the major opportunities for and threats to any organisation, and to observe standards of behaviour in such things as advertising, selling and purchasing. This still raises a number of issues for organisations.

Is it socially responsible to:

- market food with a high fat or sugar content specifically at children and offer a series of free toys?
- reduce the social impact of selling tobacco products by having an award-winning CSR policy?
- produce 'environmental friendly' weapons? For example, in 2006 the British arms manufacturer BAe Systems was reportedly designing 'environmentally friendly' weapons, including 'reduced lead' bullets, 'reduced smoke' grenades and rockets with fewer toxins.

Organisations' social responsibilities should always be set against the business context in which they operate. The examples above show that it's easy to focus only on the negative practices and ignore the positive policies of organisations in different markets. Arms suppliers and tobacco manufacturers will still have a significant impact, but how can it be reduced to a minimum?

Workplace

By providing a safe and equitable workplace, organisations can improve their employees' prosperity and standard of living. A workforce that is safe, healthy and well motivated is generally thought to be the most productive. Not only is it unethical for organisations to provide an unsafe working environment; it's also uneconomic and, in most countries, illegal.

If organisations don't invest in suitable training and safe systems of work, accident rates will tend to be higher. The financial impact of this can include:

- a loss of skilled workers
- increased downtime
- reduced productivity
- increased property damage

- increased liabilities
- higher risk of prosecution
- fines and imprisonment
- bad publicity
- reduced morale
- increased retraining costs
- increased recruitment costs
- reduced investor confidence
- increased overheads
- reduced profits.

> Prevention is not only better, but cheaper than cure ... There is no necessary conflict between humanitarianism and commercial considerations. Profits and safety are not in competition. On the contrary, safety is good business.
> *Prof Peter McKie, DuPont Corporation*

Although you can transfer some of the financial risk to an insurer, remember that the proportion of costs resulting from accidents and ill health at work that is insurable is very small. A study by the Health and Safety Executive in the UK (summarised in HSG96, *The cost of accidents at work*, 1997) suggested that the ratio of insured costs to uninsured costs may be between 1:8 and 1:36.

The tip of the accident iceberg: the relationship between insured and uninsured costs

Similar benefits can be realised through having equality-based recruitment and employment policies. Workforce diversity can help bridge gaps between the workplace and the marketplace, and open up new markets.

Organisations which mirror their customer base can enhance their image, and send a positive signal to stakeholders and potential investors.

Case study

Consider the leading soft drink manufacturer Coca-Cola. It's a market leader with a series of worldwide recognised brands, including Coke, Fanta, Sprite and Minute Maid.

This text is taken from Coca-Cola's CSR report.

As part of its global 10-year strategy for growth – The Manifesto for Growth – the Coca-Cola Company is committed to being a global citizen that makes a difference. For the Coca-Cola System in Great Britain, this means putting corporate responsibility at the heart of our business strategies.

In 2004, we introduced a new framework for managing corporate responsibility called 'Citizenship@Coca-Cola'. As part of this, we developed a series of citizenship commitments and principles which summarise our approach in four key areas or 'platforms':

Marketplace commitment

To provide products and services that meet the beverage needs of our consumers. In doing this, we provide sound and rewarding business opportunities and benefits for our customers, suppliers, distributors, and local communities.

Environment commitment

To conduct our business in ways that protect and preserve the environment and to integrate principles of environmental stewardship and sustainable development into our business decisions and processes.

Workplace commitment

To foster an open and inclusive environment where a highly motivated, productive and committed workforce drives business success through superior execution.

Community commitment

To invest time, expertise and resources to provide economic opportunity, improve the quality of life, and foster goodwill in our communities through locally relevant initiatives.

In Great Britain during 2004/05, we carried out a comprehensive review of our activities within these platforms in order to identify the key challenges we face, such as marketing responsibly to children and managing energy use, and to ensure that we are responding to these challenges appropriately.

You can see the full Coca-Cola company report at http://citizenship.coca-cola.co.uk/pdf/cr_review.pdf. An interesting and alternative view is expressed at www.waronwant.org/downloads/cocacola.pdf.

Test your thinking 11

Considering both reports, complete a review of reported performance of Coca-Cola against the areas we've discussed above. You'll need to look at both reports to do this successfully.

For each area, list examples of good practice, poor practice and impacts that you feel haven't been addressed properly. For example, under 'Community', you could cite initiatives to promote children's sport and physical activity as an example of good practice, and the continuing marketing of high-sugar drinks directly to children as an example of bad practice.

Protection

In order to make sure that basic minimum standards are in place for CSR, some key issues are already being enforced through legislation. In the UK, there is a range of legal requirements to establish basic minimum standards in a variety of settings.

Worker safety

The Health and Safety at Work etc Act 1974 and the Management of Health and Safety at Work Regulations 1999, along with significant supporting regulations, protect workers' health and safety and ensure basic welfare standards are met in workplaces.

Employment rights

The National Minimum Wage Act 1998 consolidated employees' rights to be paid at least the national minimum wage, and to receive paid annual leave. The Working Time Regulations 1998 stipulate maximum hours and minimum rest periods which employers can impose on employees.

Laws also give rights to employees not to be discriminated against on recruitment and promotion, and also set out minimum requirements for redundancy pay.

Environmental protection

A range of Acts and regulations prevent organisations from damaging the environment. The Water Resources Act 1991 makes it an offence to knowingly allow 'noxious or polluting matter' into rivers and other controlled waters.

The Environmental Protection Act 1990 places a duty of care on producers of waste to make sure it's stored securely, described accurately when transferred to a licensed waste carrier (or one with an exemption from the need to hold a licence), and disposed of at an approved site. Some wider issues, such as transport infrastructure, are also considered as part of the planning application process, particularly on larger scale projects such as supermarket developments and airport expansions. Environmental protection can play a pivotal role in the application and approval process, and therefore has a direct effect on the overall viability of the project or operation.

Construction of Terminal 5 at Heathrow Airport

At Heathrow Airport Terminal 5, BAA was aware of the significant impact the construction of a new major terminal would have. The project cost over £4 billion and included a range of mitigating measures to minimise the impact of the construction work on the environment. The planning approval process took over four years – the longest in British legal history. A construction team environmental plan was developed to tackle planning, legal and design elements, community concerns, and contingency and mitigation measures, including:

- guidance, checklists and control plans
- supplier awareness initiatives
- audits and reviews
- environmental performance indicator monitoring.

The plan tackled material use, including minimising the use of non-sustainable and toxic materials. Over 85 per cent of the waste material from the site was recovered and recycled; around 100,000 tonnes of carbon dioxide emissions were saved during design and construction; 70 per cent of the water used was from non-potable sources; and two rivers were diverted (source: BAA 2002).

Getting started

Throughout this book you should be gaining ideas and concepts that will help you to identify and tackle your CSR issues. While every organisation is different, we set out below one possible approach to implementing a CSR strategy.

Action plan

- Get senior management commitment – remember to 'sell' the benefits to your organisation. See Chapter 9 for more information on being an 'agent for change'.
- Set up a core working group. We recommend you include workforce representatives. Decide whether you want to work to a verified standard, and whether you want to seek accreditation or just use it as a good practice guide.
- Carry out a baseline review of the key issues and establish the materiality – the relevance or significance – of each issue in terms of its potential impact on stakeholders and your business. What you need to consider will vary from project to project, but typical areas will include stakeholder concerns, health and safety performance, workforce issues, supply chain, environmental footprint, community impacts and ethical trading.
- Develop a CSR strategy to tackle your key areas and define targets, policies, roles, responsibilities, training and action plans to make sure the strategy is effectively implemented.
- Establish a communication strategy to respond effectively and promptly to stakeholder issues in a transparent and sensitive way, and make sure action is taken to tackle the important issues. The strategy should also cover regular reporting to stakeholders on progress and market the CSR strategy to internal and external stakeholders.
- Review the supply chain. If your organisation is at a stage to consider a CSR strategy, it's less likely that the key issues will be internal, as you'll probably have many good practices already in place – but your supply chain might be a different matter. You'll need to develop a programme to assess suppliers' current status, develop a support and development programme and confirm their status through auditing.
- Develop key performance indicators, and regularly monitor and continually review their effectiveness and impact on your organisation.

The CSR framework we've discussed in this chapter is summarised in the figure below.

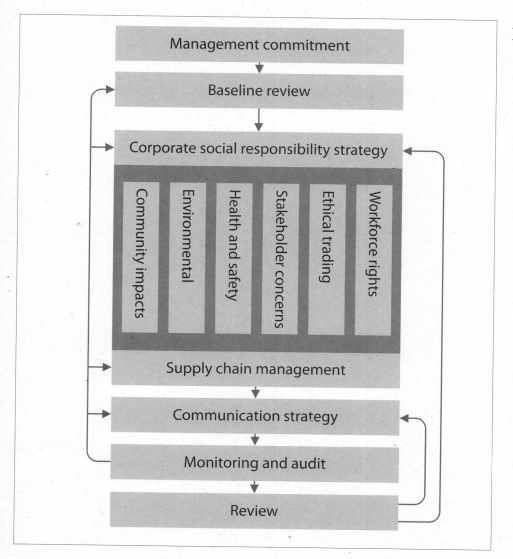

A suggested CSR framework

Management commitment

Baseline review

Corporate social responsibility strategy

Community impacts

Environmental

Health and safety

Stakeholder concerns

Ethical trading

Workforce rights

Supply chain management

Communication strategy

Monitoring and audit

Review

Chapter 6: Reporting and verifying

"I can get you as many as 100 stitchers if you need them. Of course, you'll have to pay off their peshgi* to claim them."
Pakistani factory owner

Reporting on CSR

The UK government recognises that CSR factors are important for an organisation's long-term investment and viability. This recognition was behind the proposal to introduce new reporting regulations, called the Operating and Financial Review (OFR), in 2005. However, later in 2005, the government decided to repeal the requirement on quoted companies to prepare an OFR, instead requiring them to produce a Business Review. This decision was taken in the context of the government's policy of reducing administrative burdens on organisations and took into account the evidence from consultations on narrative reporting.

The requirements for a Business Review have been added to Section 234ZZB of the Companies Act 1985, as summarised below.

1. The directors' report for a financial year must contain:
   - a fair review of the business of the organisation
   - a description of the principal risks and uncertainties facing the organisation.

2. The review must be a balanced and comprehensive analysis of:
   - the development and performance of the organisation during the financial year
   - the position of the organisation at the end of the year, in detail consistent with the size and complexity of the business.

3. The review must include the following, to the extent necessary for an understanding of the development, performance and position of the organisation's business:
   - analysis using financial key performance indicators
   - where appropriate, analysis using other key performance indicators, including information on environmental and employee matters. 'Key

---

* Money owed by workers to their masters from when they were 'bought' from their parents, or from another owner, which binds them to their master. By law, *peshgi* is banned in Pakistan, but the practice remains common. The masters call it an advance against wages, but few workers are ever able to repay the debt (see 'bonded labour' in Chapter 8).

performance indicators' means factors which can be used to measure the business's development, performance and position effectively.

If the organisation is quoted on the Stock Exchange, the auditors must state in their report whether the information given in the directors' Business Review is consistent with the accounts for the same period.

Similar regulations require large organisations that aren't listed on the Stock Exchange to produce an 'enhanced directors' report' that includes similar non-financial issues.

Verification

Clearly, in an age with almost unrestricted media and freedom for uncensored publication (particularly on the internet), any battle of claim and counter-claim regarding image and claimed and/or supposed performance could go on and on. Therefore, it's in everyone's interest that there should be some means of independently verifying organisations' claims about their standards. In the context of this book, this means verifying their claims about their CSR performance.

Specific management system standards are designed to tackle this issue. Organisations can choose to meet a set of specific criteria, and then an independently approved auditing body verifies that these standards are indeed met.

One example is the SA 8000 standard, which is a global social accountability standard for decent working conditions, developed and overseen by Social Accountability International (SAI). SA 8000 details the following principles:

- no employment of children under the age of 14 (ILO Convention 38)
- no forced labour
- a safe and healthy working environment
- the right to form trade unions
- no discrimination
- the normal working week must not exceed 48 hours
- all overtime must be reimbursed
- rates of pay must meet the legal or industry minimum and be sufficient to meet basic needs and give discretionary income
- there must be a system in place to manage and review these social issues
- air pollution: measures must be taken to reduce emissions, particularly of key pollutants, and the organisation must seek to go beyond statutory requirements

- biodiversity and habitats: the importance of biodiversity and significant habitats must be recognised and measures taken to protect and enhance them
- climate change: measures taken to monitor and reduce greenhouse gas emissions should be highlighted
- intensity of resource use: resources include energy, water, raw materials and land, and the organisation must focus on how efficiently it uses them; this criterion is linked to waste and pollution
- transport: the organisation must consider measures that reduce overall transport requirements and encourage a modal shift away from road transport (for people and freight)
- waste: measures to reduce, re-use and recycle waste
- water quality: measures to reduce discharges, particularly of key pollutants; a commitment to go beyond statutory requirements; rewarding efforts to meet objectives and targets.

As of June 2008, roughly 900,000 workers were employed in over 1,500 facilities certified to SA 8000, located in 64 countries and in 61 industrial sectors, including clothing manufacture and textiles, building materials and construction, agriculture, chemicals, cosmetics and cleaning services. The countries with the most certifications to SA 8000 are Brazil, India, China and Italy.

Other accredited management system standards which are relevant to CSR include:

- AA 1000
- ISO 14001
- BS OHSAS 18001
- ISO 26000
- Ethical Trading Initiative base code.

We'll now look at each of these in greater detail.

AA 1000
The AA 1000 series consists of principles-based standards providing the basis for improving organisations' sustainability performance. They are applicable to organisations in any sector, of any size and in any region.

The custodian of the standards, AccountAbility, says that over 150 companies have used or referred to the AA 1000 Assurance Standard in their reporting to date. These companies include Coca Cola, British American Tobacco, Vodafone, Royal Dutch Shell and Lego.

A register of applicable corporate reports, and an opportunity for readers to view them for themselves, is presented at www.corporateregister.com/search/reporters.cgi. This provides an interesting insight into the approaches adopted by some notable organisations – we recommend you visit this website.

ISO 14001

The ISO 14001 environmental management standard was developed to help organisations to minimise the negative impacts of their operations on the environment (such as adverse changes to air, land or water) and to provide a mechanism to enable compliance with applicable laws and regulations.

With origins in the earliest management standards, ISO 14001 was developed from BS 7750, and is now generally regarded as the international specification for environmental management systems. It covers:

- requirements for establishing an environmental policy
- how to determine environmental aspects and impacts of products, activities and services
- setting environmental objectives and measurable targets
- implementing and operating programmes to meet objectives, targets and significant risks
- checking and corrective action
- management review.

The ISO 14001 continual improvement cycle

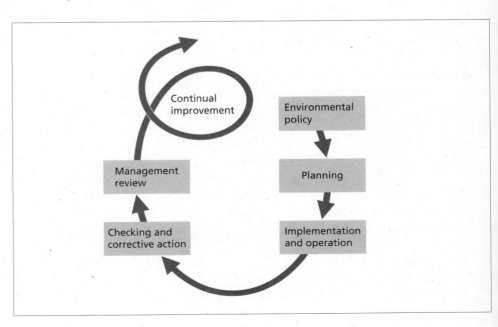

ISO 14001 is based on the classic 'Deming Wheel' Plan–Do–Check–Act approach, as shown on the opposite page.

BS OHSAS 18001

Called the Occupational Health and Safety Management System, BS OHSAS 18001 specifies requirements for a health and safety management system that enables an organisation to control its health and safety risks and to continually improve its performance.

The standard does not give specific health and safety performance criteria, nor does it give detailed specifications for designing a management system, though it is based, like ISO 14001, on the Plan-Do-Check-Act continuum.

BS OHSAS 18001:2007 is the UK's implementation of OHSAS and has the status of a British Standard. At the time of writing, there are about 16,000 certified organisations in the world.

ISO 26000

The International Organization for Standardization (ISO) has decided to launch an international standard providing guidelines for social responsibility (SR). It will be called ISO 26000, or simply ISO SR. Currently under development by a working group led by the Swedish Standards Institute and the Brazilian Association of Technical Standards, this standard is expected to be released in 2010.

ISO says that a need for organisations in both public and private sectors to behave in a socially responsible way is becoming a generalised requirement of society.

Ethical Trading Initiative base code

The Ethical Trading Initiative (ETI) was established in 1998 and aims to improve the lives of poor working people around the world. It comprises an alliance of companies, NGOs and trade unions working to promote and improve the implementation of corporate codes of practice which cover supply chain working conditions.

The base code developed by the ETI contains nine clauses which reflect the most relevant international standards on labour practices. The base code and principles of implementation have two related functions:

- they provide a basic philosophy or platform from which the ETI identifies and develops good practice
- they provide a generic standard for company performance.

The ETI base code is worth reproducing here in full:

1　Employment is freely chosen

1.1　There is no forced, bonded or involuntary prison labour.

1.2　Workers are not required to lodge 'deposits' or their identity papers with their employer and are free to leave their employer after reasonable notice.

2　Freedom of association and the right to collective bargaining are respected

2.1　Workers, without distinction, have the right to join or form trade unions of their own choosing and to bargain collectively.

2.2　The employer adopts an open attitude towards the activities of trade unions and their organisational activities.

2.3　Workers' representatives are not discriminated against and have access to carry out their representative functions in the workplace.

2.4　Where the right to freedom of association and collective bargaining is restricted under law, the employer facilitates, and does not hinder, the development of parallel means for independent and free association and bargaining.

3　Working conditions are safe and hygienic

3.1　A safe and hygienic working environment shall be provided, bearing in mind the prevailing knowledge of the industry and of any specific hazards. Adequate steps shall be taken to prevent accidents and injury to health arising out of, associated with, or occurring in the course of work, by minimising, so far as is reasonably practicable, the causes of hazards inherent in the working environment.

3.2　Workers shall receive regular and recorded health and safety training, and such training shall be repeated for new or reassigned workers.

3.3　Access to clean toilet facilities and to potable water, and, if appropriate, sanitary facilities for food storage shall be provided.

3.4　Accommodation, where provided, shall be clean, safe, and meet the basic needs of the workers.

3.5　The company observing the code shall assign responsibility for health and safety to a senior management representative.

4　Child labour shall not be used

4.1　There shall be no new recruitment of child labour.

4.2　Companies shall develop or participate in and contribute to policies and programmes which provide for the transition of any child found to be performing child labour to enable her or him to attend and remain in quality education until no longer a child; 'child' and 'child labour' being defined in the appendices.

4.3 Children and young persons under 18 shall not be employed at night or in hazardous conditions.

4.4 These policies and procedures shall conform to the provisions of the relevant ILO standards.

5 Living wages are paid

5.1 Wages and benefits paid for a standard working week meet, at a minimum, national legal standards or industry benchmark standards, whichever is higher. In any event wages should always be enough to meet basic needs and to provide some discretionary income.

5.2 All workers shall be provided with written and understandable information about their employment conditions in respect to wages before they enter employment and about the particulars of their wages for the pay period concerned each time that they are paid.

5.3 Deductions from wages as a disciplinary measure shall not be permitted nor shall any deductions from wages not provided for by national law be permitted without the expressed permission of the worker concerned. All disciplinary measures should be recorded.

6 Working hours are not excessive

6.1 Working hours comply with national laws and benchmark industry standards, whichever affords greater protection.

6.2 In any event, workers shall not on a regular basis be required to work in excess of 48 hours per week and shall be provided with at least one day off for every seven-day period on average. Overtime shall be voluntary, shall not exceed 12 hours per week, shall not be demanded on a regular basis and shall always be compensated at a premium rate.

7 No discrimination is practised

7.1 There is no discrimination in hiring, compensation, access to training, promotion, termination or retirement based on race, caste, national origin, religion, age, disability, gender, marital status, sexual orientation, union membership or political affiliation.

8 Regular employment is provided

8.1 To every extent possible work performed must be on the basis of recognised employment relationship established through national law and practice.

8.2 Obligations to employees under labour or social security laws and regulations arising from the regular employment relationship shall not be avoided through the use of labour-only contracting, sub-contracting, or home-working arrangements, or through apprenticeship schemes where there is no real intent to impart skills or provide regular employment, nor shall any such obligations be avoided through the excessive use of fixed-term contracts of employment.

9　No harsh or inhumane treatment is allowed

9.1　Physical abuse or discipline, the threat of physical abuse, sexual or other harassment and verbal abuse or other forms of intimidation shall be prohibited.

The provisions of this code constitute minimum and not maximum standards, and this code should not be used to prevent companies from exceeding these standards. Companies applying this code are expected to comply with national and other applicable law and, where the provisions of law and this Base Code address the same subject, to apply that provision which affords the greater protection.

The ETI believes that the labour standards incorporated in its base code constitute the minimum requirement for any corporate code of labour practice. Members of the ETI commit to implement the base code in their supply chains and to report annually on their progress.

Nature never deceives us: it is always we who deceive ourselves.
Jean-Jacques Rousseau (1712–1778), Swiss philosopher

Auditing and verification

The International Register of Certificated Auditors (IRCA) formally approves auditors, and requires an ongoing programme of continuing professional development for its registered auditors. Asbury & Ashwell (2007) provide a detailed review of certification and auditor registration bodies, along with their approach to risk-based auditing.

These independently verified processes were designed to resolve conflicts of fact in society, the media and elsewhere. Such processes are well established in the business-to-business procurement sector, but are (almost) unheard of in the end-user retail sector – when was the last time you checked whether the manufacturer of a product you wanted to buy was certified to SA 8000, ISO 14001 or BS OHSAS 18001?

Test your thinking 12

Nike – the company
Nike Inc produces footwear, clothing, equipment and accessory products for the sports and athletic market. It's thought to be the largest seller of such products in the world. Just about all of its products are

manufactured by independent contractors, with footwear products in particular being manufactured in developing countries.

What are the issues?

Nike has around 700 contract factories, within which around 20 per cent of the workers are creating Nike products. Conditions for these workers have been a source of heated debate, with allegations made by campaigners of poor conditions in which harassment and abuse are commonplace. Nike has sought to respond to these allegations by developing a code of conduct for all of its suppliers. In Indonesia, it was reported by Schanberg (1996) that:

> ... 30.2% of the workers had personally experienced, and 56.8% had observed, verbal abuse. An average of 7.8% of workers reported receiving unwelcome sexual comments, and 3.3% reported being physically abused. In addition, sexual trade practices in recruitment and promotion were reported by at least two workers in each of two different factories, although a subsequent investigation was unable to confirm this. 73.4% of workers are satisfied with their relationship with direct line supervisors, 67.8% are satisfied with management. The main concerns expressed by workers relate to their physical working environment.

Nike's problems also related to a site in Mexico, which had experienced serious problems leading to labour disputes. In both cases, Nike responded to the audit reports with a detailed remediation plan.

What do the critics say?

Some critics accuse Nike of abandoning countries as better pay and employment rights are developed, in favour of countries such as China, where these features are presently perhaps less important.

The photograph on the next page, widely published in 1996, shows a child in Pakistan stitching Nike footballs. Other critics have suggested that Nike should publicise conditions in all its factories, and allow independent inspection to verify them. They say that any auditing carried out by Nike should be made public. A lot of focus is given to wage rates paid by the company's suppliers. By and large, audits have found that wage rates are above the national legal minimum, but critics contend that this doesn't actually constitute a fair living wage.

What does Nike say?

Nike accuses critics of peddling inaccurate and old information. It points out that it hasn't 'abandoned countries' and that it remains in Taiwan and Korea despite the higher wages and better labour rights.

Tariq, aged 12, stitching Nike footballs in Pakistan
Photo by Marie Dorigny

Nike admits that the 1996 photograph documents what Nike describes as a 'large mistake' when they began to order footballs for the first time from a supplier in Pakistan. They now operate stitching centres which are confirmed not to be using child labour.

Nike believes that sharing factory locations with independent third parties on a confidential basis enables them to monitor their supply chain properly. As for wage rates, the company feels that establishing what constitutes a 'fair' wage is by no means as easy as its critics would have the public believe, and disparages the constant quoting of wage rates in US dollar equivalents, when these are meaningless given the different costs of living in the countries concerned.

Nike is also dismayed at how it has become the principal target of campaigners in this area. The company asks campaigners to look at its competitors as well and find out how many of them have taken the kind of measures that Nike has over the last few years.
Source: www.mallenbaker.net

This case study raises several questions:

1. What are the key CSR issues for Nike?

2. Do you think Nike has gone far enough in its supplier auditor programme?

3. What else could Nike do in this regard?

4. What are the possible reasons Nike could have for not publishing the reports?

5. If Nike published the reports, do you think that pressure groups would believe them?

6. Why or why not?

7. Do you think pressure groups focus more on companies that claim to be good, rather than those who claim (or seem) to do nothing?

Auditing and validating claims of good deeds and on-the-ground performance is likely to remain an issue for some time. It would help to have agreed common approaches, such as those noted in this chapter, backed up as necessary by a legal framework requiring organisations to maintain similar performance standards overseas as they do at home. We look forward to seeing developments in this area in the coming years.

The era of procrastination, of half-measures, of soothing and baffling expedients, of delays, is coming to a close. In its place, we are entering a period of consequences.
Sir Winston Churchill (1874–1965), later UK Prime Minister, in a speech in 1936

Chapter 7: The case against CSR

"What has never been doubted has never been proven."
Denis Diderot (1713–1784)

Around the world, some individuals and some organisations believe that CSR is an unnecessary burden. They believe that the principal reason companies are in business is to make profits for their shareholders. They also believe that addressing issues commonly connected to CSR should be the preserve of national governments and environmental (and other) charities, not private companies.

In today's tough financial climate, organisations need to focus on their core activities. As an agent of CSR, you need to be able to understand these arguments and develop strategies to deal with stakeholders' concerns – whether you think they're legitimate or not. Take, for example, the headline 'Recycling fiasco' in the *Mail on Sunday* on 4 January 2009. The article outlines how councils are having to pay substantial storage costs for recyclables as their value has fallen on world markets. Stakeholders will rightly question why they should be paying higher Council Tax and business rates to store this material – why can't it just be sent to landfill?

In this chapter, we'll ask you to consider questions and case studies so that you can develop your arguments in favour of doing the right thing.

Test your thinking 13
Consider each of the following arguments against CSR and prepare a positive response:

1. Businesses exist to make profit for their shareholders – not to support society.

2. It's the responsibility of the politicians to deal with all this stuff. It's not up to businesses to get involved.

3. Struggling businesses are just trying to survive hard times – they can't afford to do this.

Here are some key themes and possible responses to these questions.

1. Businesses exist to make profit for their shareholders – not to support society

CSR is about balancing social, environmental and economic needs. Companies that are aware of the social climate can adapt to it, building customer loyalty and increasing market share. Many CSR factors are also about reducing overheads such as resource consumption and energy use, and harnessing in-house potential through raising staff morale.

Ethical trading with suppliers and customers will also increase the long-term viability and success of the organisation, through more closely aligned objectives, a more secure supply base and bringing the benefits to the whole of your supply chain.

2. It's the responsibility of the politicians to deal with all this stuff. It's not up to businesses to get involved

Politicians are representatives of the community, including businesses. Many companies spend considerable time and money seeking to influence public policy in their area of interest. That area of interest can range far and wide – from international treaties on climate change, through to domestic policies on health (such as those relating to smoking) or transport. The lobbying activities of companies in these areas show that they do have a role, whether they like it or not.

CSR is not just about obeying the law and paying taxes; it's about managing risk and reputation, and investing in community resources on which you depend.

3. Struggling businesses are just trying to survive hard times – they can't afford to do this

If a company is struggling (and not just whining!), it's even more important to build a competitive advantage. If this same company ignores CSR issues, it's putting itself at an even greater risk – it may end up paying to clean up pollution or damage, being prosecuted and fined, or attracting unwelcome attention from environmental or human rights pressure groups and the media.

Losing or missing out on skilled employees by discriminating on the basis of race, sex, age or sexual orientation isn't good for business either. Well-qualified individuals have a choice about where they earn their living. Will they work for an irresponsible company?

An irresponsible organisation also risks losing an increasingly large group of customers who prefer to purchase sustainable goods and services.

All of these negative impacts contribute to the economic and environmental downturn of an area, leading to more recruitment problems. If it doesn't optimise efficiency, the organisation also becomes less competitive as it's forced to spend more than it would otherwise have needed on manufacturing, disposal of waste, energy and other resources.

Case study: BP Amoco – is CSR a problem or an opportunity?

BP Amoco is one of the largest companies in the world, with a capitalisation of $232 billion in January 2007. It has a financial turnover which dwarfs that of some small countries. As a petroleum company, it's directly linked to the exploration and production of products from fossil fuels, which in turn are linked to major global environmental challenges.

Perhaps more than any other company, BP has achieved a high profile through its determination to completely re-orientate its business to adapt to the needs of a more sustainable society. With its major – and controversial – rebranding and its commitment to become a sustainable energy company rather than simply a petroleum company, it's inspired and impressed some, and irritated others.

The pioneer of this repositioning was BP's former chairman, Sir John Browne, who established himself as one of the most thoughtful business leaders by taking a lead in CSR.

The company

BP is a leading petroleum company. Its main businesses are onshore and offshore exploration and production of oil and natural gas, refining and marketing, and petrochemicals. In addition, the company has a solar energy business which is one of the world's largest manufacturers of photovoltaic modules and systems.

What are the issues?

There are very few aspects of how a company behaves as a corporate citizen that don't apply to a company of the size and nature of BP. The most significant of these is the sheer environmental impact. This is felt not only in the extraction of petroleum, and the energy used in BP's own operations, but also, and more significantly, through climate change caused by the company's customers using its products.

A company with such extensive operations in developing countries also needs to be careful about its approach to human rights and ethical business practices. BP will have significant impacts on local communities –

both as a huge employer and through the nature of its on-the-ground operations. It should seriously expect to seek to reduce any negative impacts there, and to invest meaningfully in those communities.

BP, as a global player, is immensely powerful. It has no democratic legitimacy, but is often better able to lead on the social development of the planet than national governments. This is a dilemma it needs to handle carefully.

What do the critics say?
Critics point out that BP's claim to be a global leader in producing the cleanest-burning fossil fuel (natural gas) is only an incremental improvement over oil at best, and a distraction from getting away from fossil fuels at worst. BP, they claim, has co-opted the language of the environmentalist without a real commitment to deliver. As for BP's assertion that it's now the largest producer of solar energy in the world, they point out that achieving this number one position was trivially easy. It acquired the Solarex solar energy corporation at a cost of $45 million – a minute fraction of the $26.5 billion it spent on buying Amoco to increase its petroleum capacity. In fact, it's been widely speculated that the company spent more on its new 'eco-friendly' logo than it has so far on solar energy investments!

What does BP say?
BP says that it recognises the significant environmental and social challenges faced by the world in the 21st century. BP believes it can, and should, play a part in addressing and resolving many of the issues associated with sustainable development. BP also accepts that while the company can be part of the solution, it can't and shouldn't be the whole solution. Governments, companies and society must find effective ways of working together.

Alongside the standard financial figures, BP reports its own greenhouse gas and other emissions, spillages, employee satisfaction, days lost through injury at work, and community investment across the world.

On the question of the impact of petroleum use, Sir John Browne argued that hydrocarbons are crucial to the economic success of the world, while renewable energy holds great long-term potential. For the moment, however, there are no viable substitutes for hydrocarbons. Those companies, he said, that can supply the resources that the world needs, and do so in ways that meet public concern about the environment, are well placed to deliver exceptional returns to their shareholders.

BP's company policy statements commit the company to ambitious and wide-ranging business principles. The company's reporting seeks to illustrate how the company is meeting these commitments in a way that supports the profitability of the business.

Find out for yourself by looking at the two following sources of information, and then answer the questions beneath.

1. BP's website dealing with key CSR issues can be found at www.bp.com/productlanding.do?categoryId=4520&contentId=7014704. BP's latest report and policy statement is at www.bp.com/downloads/458/BP_Rev_Complete.pdf.

2. There's an alternative perspective on BP's profits and environmental costs at www.guardian.co.uk/oil/story/0,,1707701,00.html.

Test your thinking 14

1. What do you consider to be the key CSR issues for BP Amoco?

2. Has BP identified CSR as a problem or an opportunity?

3. How well does the corporate reporting tackle the main issues?

4. What do you think are the key motivating factors behind BP's rebranding?

5. Does BP answer the critics' concerns?

6. Do you think companies such as BP are a net contributor or consumer in society?

7. Would you purchase BP's products as a matter of choice over any other competitors?

8. Do you think that *The Guardian*'s article is pro- or anti-BP?

This time, we haven't provided any sample answers, because there are few right or wrong ones! The idea of the exercise is to encourage you to elaborate your thoughts and ideas on CSR. We urge you to look at other organisations from a similar perspective – perhaps starting with your own. We think that a competent practitioner should know the arguments against CSR as well as for it.

In the years 1846 to date, the ten hottest years on record have been in the last 14 years.
Paramount Film Classics, 'An Inconvenient Truth', Cannes Film Festival 2006

Chapter 8: Issues in the supply chain

"With great power, there must also come great responsibility!"
Spider-Man (attributed to Stan Lee, Amazing Fantasy *No. 15, August 1962, Marvel Comics*)

"Do, or do not. There is no 'try'."
Yoda, in 'The Empire Strikes Back'

The core principle of CSR concerns managing our relations with others to minimise the negative and maximise the positive. One of the most direct ways that any organisation can interact with others is through its supply chain.

A supply chain is all the links in a product's life cycle that bring the product or service to the customer. This includes the raw materials consumed by your organisation, all the manufacturing and quality control processes, delivery to the point of consumption and subsequent disposal. This supply chain creates a 'cradle-to-grave' continuum. All organisations in a supply chain are linked, and they depend on one another in order to operate. The managers of these relationships should focus on two key directions:

- purchasing or procurement, looking upstream
- sales and customer service, concentrating on the downstream processes.

In this chapter, we'll look at how suppliers and customers could choose – or be influenced – to interact in positive ways with your organisation, and how their decisions can be associated with positive or negative outcomes. We'll consider the responsibilities your organisation has within its supply chain, and the benefits of promoting CSR among your supply chain contacts.

The essence of business
Organisations generally exist to provide goods and services. Businesses aim to make a profit from doing this. Providing goods and services involves interactions between two or more parties, where money (or other reimbursement) is exchanged as payment for the supply of the goods or services. Organisations usually need to buy a wide range of goods and services to operate – eg raw materials, electricity and water. However, as this provision could be open to abuse, the concept of a contract or legally binding promise – bound by the rules of offer, acceptance and consideration – has been developed and enforced through the ages. The principle of a contract is that a supplier of goods or services agrees to

deliver products of the right quantity and right quality at the right time in exchange for the agreed right price.

> In my culture … a good agreement is self-enforcing because both parties go away smiling and are happy to see that each of us is smiling. If one smiles and the other scowls, the agreement will not stick, lawyers or no lawyers.
> *Charles Handy*, The Empty Raincoat *(Arrow Books, 1994)*

This pure capitalism has to have its boundaries. We should remember that individuals will try to gain profit at the expense of others – some legally but others illegally – even within this framework of contract and ownership. There is often significant potential for one party to gain an upper hand over another, and you should question whether your organisation abuses its purchasing power.

Let's consider what is, for most people, the most abhorrent trade – slavery. In Chapter 2, we outlined the abolition of slavery in the UK and then in the British colonies in the 19th century. It's also prohibited by:

- the Universal Declaration of Human Rights, 1948
- the UN Supplementary Convention on the Abolition of Slavery, 1956.

But slavery is still practised. In bonded labour, workers are deceived into taking a loan for immigration, transit or medical care. They're then forced to work long hours, seven days a week, for up to 365 days a year. They receive basic food and shelter as 'payment' for their work, but may never pay off the loan, which can be passed down for generations. Forced labour affects people who are illegally recruited by individuals, governments or political parties and forced to work – sometimes under threats of violence or other penalties.

In slavery by descent, people are either born into a slave class or are from an ethnic, economic or other group that society views as suited to being used as slave labour.

Trafficking involves the transport and/or trade of people from one area to another for the purpose of forcing them into slavery, including the sex trade. While we trust that it's unlikely that anyone reading this book will be involved in trafficking women into bonded prostitution, your organisation may be supporting other human or environmental bad practices through your supply chain selections. Think about these questions:

- How, and by whom, were the clothes you're wearing now made?
- Are you wearing jewellery? In what conditions was the gold mined?

- Do you drink coffee? Was the price you paid for it fair to the producer?
- Does your paper come from recycled or sustainably managed sources?
- What are working conditions like in your suppliers' premises? Are they safe and healthy?
- Are your suppliers or customers causing pollution?

Would you want your brand showing here?

Consider the allegations made by farmers against Tesco:

Farmers accuse Tesco of putting them out of business

At Tesco's annual meeting yesterday, one farmer from Lincolnshire said he was losing 2p on every litre of milk that left his farm due to low prices imposed by Tesco and other supermarkets. "We need a fair farm gate price for milk so that farmers could get a fair return on their investment," he said.

Tesco Chief Executive Terry Leahy said the company was doing all it could in the circumstances to help farmers to be successful because the company had a vested interest in keeping a healthy supply chain.

He said Tesco tried to source products from local domestic markets instead of imports wherever possible.

But he said the firm's actions were at least partly governed by factors outside its control such as exchange rates, government policy and movement in global agricultural prices.

Source: The Western Mail, 19 June 2004

The UK government has since introduced a code of conduct for large supermarkets after it was shown that they were distorting the market. This demonstrates that even (or especially) the largest organisations need to consider their responsibilities to supply chains.

Price

Traditionally, many organisations have focused on obtaining goods and services for the cheapest possible price. Profit is basically derived by the formula:

$$Profit = value\ of\ sales - cost\ of\ purchases$$

However, many organisations established that the cheapest price and the best price are two different things – that price wasn't the sole ingredient in a good contract. Value and cheapest price are two different parameters. Consider a t-shirt that's made using child labour, cheap cotton and polluting dyes, manufactured in sweatshop conditions and sold for 99p, but which shrinks and fades after the first wash. Is this good value? Several pressure groups recognise that much of our consumption is fuelled by our lifestyles and suggest that it's the responsibility of large multinational companies to drive change into their supply chains wherever they're located. As consumers, we must consider the price, manufacturing standards, environmental good practice and quality when we assess good value.

The recognition of the responsibility of multinationals to supply chains helped to develop the 'UN Global Compact', which incorporates 10 core principles of CSR. The table on the next page provides a summary of these principles.

Test your thinking 15

Consider your organisation's suppliers and contractors, their conduct and your procurement processes.

1. To what degree does your organisation actively uphold, enforce and promote each of the 10 principles listed?

2. Could your organisation go further towards adopting them?

Human rights principles	
Principle 1	Businesses should support and respect the protection of internationally proclaimed human rights
Principle 2	Businesses should ensure that their own operations are not complicit in human rights abuses
Labour principles	
Principle 3	Businesses should uphold the freedom of association and the effective recognition of the right to collective bargaining
Principle 4	Businesses should uphold the elimination of forced or compulsory labour
Principle 5	Businesses should uphold the effective abolition of child labour
Principle 6	Businesses should uphold the elimination of discrimination in respect of employment and occupation
Environment principles	
Principle 7	Businesses should support a precautionary approach to environmental challenges
Principle 8	Businesses should undertake initiatives to promote greater environmental responsibility
Principle 9	Businesses should encourage the development and diffusion of environmentally friendly technologies
The anti-corruption principle	
Principle 10	Businesses should work against all forms of corruption, including extortion and bribery

A summary of the principles of the UN Global Compact

We'll now look at some issues that may influence your answers to these questions.

Choosing suppliers

In addition to value for money, will you seek to further your corporate responsibility objectives through your purchasing activity and supplier relationships? Will you use ethical criteria to exclude or positively discriminate in favour of certain suppliers? Will you support initiatives that aim to increase the number of diverse (eg ethnic-minority owned, women-owned) businesses that supply goods and services to your organisation? You may also wish to consider measures to make sure that small businesses are given fair consideration.

Conduct during procurement

This refers to the way your staff conduct business – how goods and services are bought on behalf of the organisation. Are your staff encouraged and supported to act with integrity, and in line with your organisation's ethical values when establishing and maintaining supplier relationships? Do you insist that your suppliers' bills are paid on time, or that offers of gifts and hospitality are registered? How do you prevent conflicts of interest? If you work for a large company, are you concerned to be judged as a fair customer by your suppliers? Do you have policies on dependency, or on transparency regarding tendering, or on engagement when contract terms are not met, changed or are being wound down?

Your supplier's practices

Are you clear about the extent of your organisation's responsibility down and across the supply chain? What do you expect of your suppliers? Do you impose social and environmental standards on them? Do you seek to influence their policies and practices or offer them assistance to improve?

Sustainable procurement

The concept of incorporating CSR into the purchasing process is called 'sustainable procurement'. Sustainable procurement is the inclusion of environmental, social and economic factors in purchasing decisions, so that the long-term viability and maximum value of the goods or services can be obtained for the organisation, the community and the environment. It involves reviewing the organisation's procurement policies to widen the scope from purely best price or best quality to include elements from the CSR agenda.

Sustainable procurement seeks to recognise, and emphasise, that as the buyer, you have a huge degree of discretion over your choice of suppliers. This discretion not only includes your choice of the people and organisations you trade with, but also goes beyond this first-tier supply into the whole supply chain – how and where they obtain their resources. Sustainable procurement highlights that it's not just your choice but also your responsibility to make sure that your supply chain is well managed and operates on a socially and environmentally sound basis, not purely an economic one.

The purchasing decision should include gathering information on the impact of the organisation's suppliers, including their areas of environmental impact and their record on employment rights and ethical trading. There are numerous benefits for organisations which promote environmental issues in the supplier chain:

- Cost savings. If you encourage suppliers to reduce waste, use fewer resources and be more energy efficient, they can produce goods at a lower cost. One organisation implemented a returnable packaging scheme, eliminating 21,720 cardboard cartons, with annual savings of £7,000 and 15 tonnes of waste.
- Supplier loyalty. Developing partnership working reduces costs and CSR impacts, builds the relationship with suppliers and helps in all sectors.
- Minimising corporate risk. If you've verified that your suppliers are suitable, it minimises the chance that a major social or environmental incident or prosecution will affect the supply.
- Demonstrating good management. Developing the supply chain well illustrates that the organisation is well managed and encourages shareholders to invest. It also tells you what your suppliers' management style is, demonstrating how forward-thinking and adaptive they can be.
- Accreditation and certification. SA 8000, ISO 14001 and Global Compact each require organisations to identify their aspects and their controls, including contractors and suppliers. They should develop improvement objectives for significant impacts.* If an organisation wants to gain accreditation, it will generally need to include a supplier development programme.
- Competitive advantage. CSR provides opportunities to increase market share and to open new markets. Customers and shareholders alike are increasingly aware of organisations' CSR credentials, and base their buying decisions on what they find out. This may include the impact of the life cycle of the product.
- Brand protection. For some organisations, 'environment' is a component of the brand, eg Body Shop. For others, bad publicity on CSR issues could affect the brand image – for example, Coca Cola has experienced bad publicity about its alleged consumption of scarce water supplies in India.[†]
- Ethical duty. Particularly for public sector organisations, CSR management demonstrates that the organisation considers the needs of its community in its procurement policy.

---

* The terms 'aspect' and 'impact' are used here in the meanings given in ISO 14001:2004. An aspect is 'an element of an organisation's activities, products or services that can interact with the environment', while an impact is 'any change to the environment, whether adverse or beneficial, wholly or partially resulting from an organisation's activities, products or services'.

† For more information, see www.corpwatch.org/article.php?id=7508.

Sustainable
procurement
guide
*Adapted from the
Environment
Agency,
www.environment-
agency.gov.uk/
commondata/
103599/
spg_517077.doc*

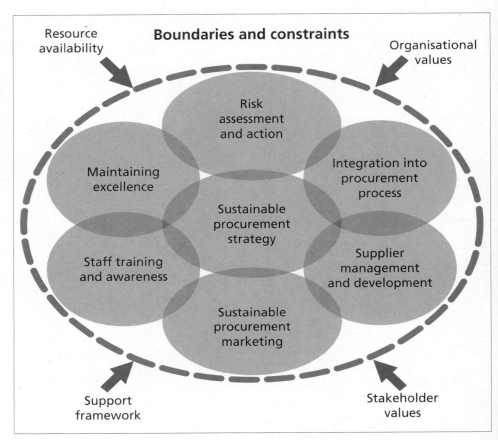

The Environment Agency in the UK has developed a sustainable procurement strategy focusing on six key elements, as illustrated in the figure above.

The first stage of this sustainable procurement strategy is to understand your aspects and impacts. As with any risk management system, the initial milestone is to be aware and assess the magnitude of the effects your organisation is having socially, environmentally and economically on a local and global scale. The scale and nature of your organisation's operation will determine the depth, approach and comprehensiveness of your review. In this chapter, we're focusing on supply chain issues, but this could also include the impacts of the operations and outputs of your organisation.

If any system is to be embedded in the operations and culture of an organisation, right from the start you should consider how it'll be integrated into the current structures and procedures of the organisation.

If sustainable procurement is to become part of considerations at the purchasing stage, you need to review how you currently assess your suppliers, and how much weight you'll give to CSR over (say) price or reliable delivery. In developing your procurement strategy you need to strike the right balance. If CSR is weighted too lightly, this will not bring about the significant change you want to encourage.

Supplier management can be tackled in two key ways. The first is to incorporate CSR considerations at the specification level, where appropriate, using a scoring method to include the benefits to the environment and communities in the selection process. The second is to encourage suppliers to improve the CSR footprint of the goods or services they supply to you. It's important to consider our approach with our suppliers – do we expect them to change overnight? Most people think not – this wouldn't be a reasonable approach to CSR, however desirable it might be. Instead, we probably need to nurture them over time to gain sustained benefits.

One of the best methods is to support a dialogue with the intention of identifying 'win–win' situations. Try not to work on a 'stick' approach – focus on the positives that improved CSR will bring to both organisations. Highlight why you're doing it, and the pressures and benefits. Many organisations operate a scored procurement process. CSR can be integrated into this process with an appropriate weighting. Suppliers can be moved onto a supplier development list and supported if they're significant for your organisation. If your organisation doesn't have a formal procurement process, then this could be an ideal time to find out what the right strategy would be for you. Would a little more time spent at the purchasing stage save problems further down the line?

Other methods of supplier management include:

- questionnaire samples to ascertain suppliers' current status
- developing a code of conduct
- developing purchasing checklists
- making a positive effort to support voluntary and charity organisations through, for example, buying goods and services from them
- benchmarking your supplier chain against those of other suitable organisations.

Sustainable procurement marketing – how can we make the most of the good work we're doing?

It's important to celebrate your successes and show others the benefits of a sustainable procurement policy. Initially, the approach of introducing policy is critical, rather than dictating the process. You need to show how this will be useful to others' organisations and demonstrate the range of advantages. You need to show a partnership approach, remembering that suppliers are as entitled to benefit from the principles of CSR just as much as the general community. By negotiating with and influencing them, you're more likely to champion change.

Clearly there comes a situation where a supplier organisation must either comply with your core principles, or not be used.

> It is a mistake to isolate 'greening the supply chain' as something completely different. It should be presented and received as one of the many customer expectations (in addition to price, performance, quality etc). If you treat it as a new and separate conversation, it may look more difficult than it needs to be. Given the natural tendency to resist change, there is no need to make this any larger than it needs to be as long as you are able to get the performance improvements you are after.
> *Ben Packard, Director of Environmental Affairs, Starbucks*

Staff competence

If you're to ask staff to develop in their roles and to incorporate CSR into their working life (and home life – see Chapter 9), you need to make sure that they have an understanding of the key concepts, the benefits and their individual roles in the organisation's approach to CSR.

While on one level, the basic concepts are welcomed by many, incorporating it into work-based decisions can be more of a challenge. Ensuring an effective sustainable procurement strategy needs specifiers, influencers, budget holders, buyers and senior management all to understand their roles and the impacts their decisions can have on CSR.

Maintaining excellence

Once you've set your policy, taken a benchmark, and assessed your suppliers, how can you continue to improve and promote your CSR goals? The first stage is to verify your current position through auditing; this is dealt with in more depth in Chapter 6.

Once an audit programme is in place, the next stage is to consider how and to what extent your organisation should support improvements in your supply chain. This will clearly depend on a wide range of factors, including:

- public or private sector
- size of organisation
- policy or belief in CSR
- resources available

- significance of risks or impacts
- market sector
- competition
- media interest
- supplier base
- good practice information availability.

It's important to recognise the wider benefits of the supplier development programme so that all the costs can be considered. Hosting a supplier development workshop may also build better relationships to aid the understanding of operations from both the supplier's and client's perspective. This is a simple event or series of events that encourage communication and sharing of ideas to solve problems that are common to the supply chain, such as logistic or manufacturing issues.

Typical improvement ideas for suppliers can include:

- knowledge exchange workshops (where best practice is shared), training and information
- shared ideas and common goals
- practical solutions, such as shared waste minimisation programmes, energy efficiency, returnable packaging systems, transport solutions, life cycle assessment, fair trade concepts, shared sustainable product research
- long-term partnership planning to support the viability of all organisations in the supply chain.

Once you've established your strategy, remember to bring it to the attention of your current and prospective clients.

Test your thinking 16

Consider your own organisation, and the suggestions outlined in the sustainable procurement strategy model, and answer these questions:

1. Who are your key suppliers?

2. Which of these suppliers is most likely to have a major CSR impact?

3. How could CSR be integrated into your current purchasing polices?

4. Who makes or influences purchasing decisions in your organisation?

5. What information, skills and training would these people need to incorporate CSR principles into the decisions they make?

6. How could you market a sustainable procurement strategy to your suppliers?

7. What are the main barriers to starting now and how could you overcome them?

8. How could you help your suppliers improve their CSR performance?

Whether you work with a large company or public sector body with direct impacts, or a small to medium-sized enterprise within a supply chain, the pressure is on you to ensure good practice throughout your lives. The point of CSR is to get you to consider your impacts on others and the environment. After your own operations, the contractors and suppliers you select are the most direct influences you have. Health and safety legislation and product liability regulations recognise the duty you have for your supply chain; when will you acknowledge your responsibility for the purchasing decisions your organisation makes?

We cannot say we love the land and then take steps to destroy it.
Pope John Paul II (1920–2005)

Chapter 9: Personal social responsibility

"No man is an island, entire of itself.... Any man's death diminishes me, because I am involved in mankind; and therefore never send to know for whom the bell tolls; it tolls for thee."
John Donne (1572–1631), Devotions upon emergent occasions, Meditation XVII

I may be only one person, but I can be one person who makes a difference.
Vadra Francene Groce, aged 10, of Bowling Green, Kentucky (from exhibition at EPCOT Park, Florida)

So far in this book, we've looked at the role of the organisation in examining its responsibilities to stakeholders and developing a programme to mitigate its negative effects. However, as society and organisations are made up of individuals, we should consider how our personal decisions affect the wider society. Our purchasing decisions are one of the strongest powers we have, whether in our home life or at work. The selection we make at the checkout is the ultimate demonstration of the level of respect we have for workers we may never meet, the ethics we support and supply chains we condone. And it's not just what we choose to buy – our other actions, such as how much we recycle and what we turn off, also have an impact on the world around us.

Personal social responsibility (PSR) is an important component in any CSR programme as it recognises that, as individuals, we're usually the end users of the products or services we've been discussing so far in this book. It's important that we take individual responsibility for the impacts associated with those products and services. When we buy something, we're supporting and implicitly approving of all of the actions in the supply chain that brought that product to us. If that product or service used child labour, forced people to work in poor conditions or caused significant pollution, hasn't that all been done on our behalf for our purchase, to satisfy our needs and desires?

In this chapter, we consider what an individual can do to minimise their personal social impact, and we highlight how an individual can become an agent for change within their own sphere of influence. We can all live behind the theory that it's somebody else's job; complain that our own actions won't make a significant difference; and point to others who are worse than us. But change requires action! Action requires individuals to make a conscious effort to alter their current behaviour patterns. History reminds us of the individuals who have made a difference for good or bad – Nelson Mandela, Mahatma Gandhi, Mother Teresa, Bob Geldof, Bill Gates, Adolf Hitler or Osama bin Laden. All have changed our world to a greater or lesser extent. You too can be the agent for change in your life, household, organisation or community.

If you're to make a difference, you need to understand how to instigate and sustain change. It's easy to get enthusiastic about a new project at the start, but how can you make sure that it results in lasting changes over the longer term, and that you don't return to your old ways when the novelty wears off? Being an agent for change either in your own life or in other people's behaviour requires effort, tenacity and ardour. Effective change can be supported by seven simple and logical steps:

1. Focus on what you can change, not what you can't. At the start, or when times get tough, it's easy to get distracted by focusing on areas that you have little or no control over. You need to be realistic and spend your efforts on your own sphere of activity and influence.

2. Identify barriers. With any programme of change, there are always challenges to face. By identifying them early on, and by considering options and coping strategies, they don't have to derail your progress if or when they crop up.

3. Set realistic targets. We all work better when we have something to aim for and to plot progress against. By considering what you need or want to achieve, you can make sure you channel your time and effort in the right direction. And don't be too optimistic about what can be achieved.

4. Easy wins. We all get motivated by good news! A sense of achievement can come from building in attainable milestones early in the plan. This helps to develop momentum more quickly, reinforce behaviour change and support your progress towards the long-term objectives.

5. Monitor your progress. It's important to develop some simple monitoring measures to make sure that progress is kept on track.

6. Look for the positives. Many people concentrate on the things they could have done better. This can create a negative outlook, reinforcing past behaviour patterns. Look at what you have positively achieved and how the new plan is making a difference.

7. Celebrate each success! When targets are achieved, reward yourself.

The fact that you're reading this chapter shows your commendable desire to make that change. So – ask yourself now: what practical steps can you take right away to make a difference?

Celebrate success

Look for positive

Monitor progress

Easy wins

Target setting

Identify barriers

Focus

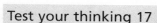

Seven steps to PSR change

Test your thinking 17

Considering the influence you have in your personal life, at work and in your community, what can you do to optimise your personal social responsibility? Use the list below as a guide.

1. Your personal life
   - What do you buy?
   - How do you live?
   - What do you use?
   - How do you travel? (When you must travel less than 1 mile; to work; to city centres; on holiday?)
   - What do you tell your children?
   - What do you tell your friends?
   - What do you learn?
   - What do you throw away?

2. Workplace
   - What decisions do you make at work?
   - Who can you influence?
   - What decisions can you influence?
   - What do you use in your work?
   - What do you throw away?

3. Community
- Do you vote?
- How you do vote?
- Do you do any formal or informal voluntary work?
- How can you help with the skills you have (or could learn)?
- Who do you talk to and network with?
- Who do you know who is active in your community?
- What can one person do?

These ideas are all possibilities. Not every suggestion will apply to everyone, but we can all do more than we do now.

Get informed – make sure that you're aware of what you're buying, and what the current issues are.

While there's a confusing amount of information on CSR issues, the simple test is to buy products that you believe, in all good faith, have been produced with the aim of reducing the negative impact on those who produce and supply them, wildlife and the environment.

Use labels to choose products that have a lower impact on the environment – for example, fair trade products, energy efficient appliances and cars, and sustainable fish. Using labels to buy sustainable wood and peat-free compost will protect important natural habitats that help balance climate change effects. If you're unsure, the information age means it's easy to find out!

In order to help you with this process you need to get 'labelwise'. Logos and labels are there to help us to quickly recognise those products that meet a certain standard. At an organisational level, it may be that the company is certificated to an accredited standard (see Chapter 6). But what about the everyday consumer? What information is on the label, and what do these labels mean?

Labelling

Fair trade

Fair trade is about better prices, decent working conditions, local sustainability, and fair terms of trade for farmers and workers in the developing world. By requiring companies to pay sustainable prices (which must never fall lower than the market price), Fair trade addresses the injustices of conventional trade, which traditionally discriminates against the

poorest, weakest producers. It enables them to improve their position and have more control over their lives.
Fair Trade Foundation

For more information, contact the Fair Trade Foundation, www.fairtrade. org.uk.

Organic

To many people, 'organic' means made without man-made chemicals. However, within the EU, in order for a product to be marketed as organic it must meet particular certification standards. These are implemented in the UK under the Organic Products Regulations 2004, through the Compendium of UK Organic Standards.

The Soil Association has added to these standards and developed a logo that is widely used. The product showing the label must meet a range of agricultural, environmental, food processing and social principles.

The Soil Association's agricultural principles are to:

- produce food of high quality in sufficient quantity
- work within natural systems and cycles throughout all levels from the soil to plants and animals
- maintain the long-term fertility and biological activity of soils
- treat livestock ethically, meeting their physiological and behavioural needs
- respect regional, environmental, climatic and geographic differences and (appropriate) practices that have evolved in response to them.

Its environmental principles are to:

- foster biodiversity and protect sensitive habitats and landscape features
- maximise use of renewable resources and recycling
- minimise pollution and waste.

Its food processing principles are to:

- minimise processing, consistent with the food in question
- maximise information on processing methods and ingredients.

Its social principles are to:

- provide a fair and adequate quality of life, work satisfaction and working environment

- develop ecologically responsible production, processing and distribution chains, emphasising local systems.

Recycled *vs* recyclable

Many products show the 'three chasing arrows' recycling logo, called the 'Möbius loop'. There are a number of similar recycling logos, and it's important to understand the different meanings:

This symbol denotes that the material is able to be recycled. It may be produced from virgin material but, as the consumer, you can recycle it. Until you do, there's little benefit to the environment.

If you buy recyclable materials, it's vital that you do indeed recycle them, in order to achieve the intended benefits of reducing resource use and cutting landfill waste.

The recycling symbol with a single figure inside (ie without a per cent sign) indicates a plastic recycling classification to help in sorting material after collection and before processing. The figure on the opposite page explains the numbers and abbreviations.

Items made from recycled materials are usually labelled with a different Möbius loop marking. This time, it has a percentage figure inside. This indicates the percentage of the product's material that has been recycled – this shows obvious environmental benefits. These items can also themselves be recycled.

The 'crossed-out wheelie bin' symbol means that the electrical product carrying it complies with EN 50419, and is recyclable. If you bought it after 13 August 2005, you can take it back to the store where you bought it for recycling. (You're responsible for appropriately disposing of electrical appliances bought before this date, but some retailers will accept these older products for recycling, especially if you're buying a replacement from them.)

Forest Stewardship Council

Products displaying this mark are made from wood that comes from well-managed forests and has been certified according to the Forest Stewardship Council standards by independent organisations.

This mark may be displayed with a percentage figure to show how much of the materials come from recycled sources. But unlike with the standard recycling symbol, products without the percentage figure can also be considered as having a lower environmental impact.

Plastic recycling classifications

PETE	**Polyethylene terephthalate ethylene** PETE goes into soft drink, juice, water, detergent and cleaner bottles. Also used for cooking and peanut butter jars	PP	**Polypropylene** PP goes into caps, discs, syrup bottles, yogurt tubs, straws and film packaging
HDPE	**High density polyethylene** HDPE goes into milk and water jugs, bleach, shampoo and detergent bottles, plastic bags, motor oil bottles and butter tubs	PS	**Polystyrene** PS goes into meat trays, egg boxes, plates, cutlery, take-away containers and clear trays
PVC	**Polyvinyl chloride** PVC goes into window cleaner, cooking oil and detergent bottles. Also used for peanut butter jars and water jugs	OTHER	**Other** Includes resins not mentioned above or combinations of plastics
LDPE	**Low density polyethylene** LDPE goes into plastic bags and grocery sacks, dry cleaning bags, flexible film packaging and some bottles		

Other symbols

A common symbol on packaging in the UK is the green dot (*der grüne Punkt*). This has no direct environmental significance but indicates the manufacturer has paid into a packaging recovery system in Germany.

However, it's not all about the labels. There are also simple steps you can take to reduce the impact of the items that you buy, such as buying from local suppliers where possible, buying fresh and in-season food only, and buying only what you need.

Consider what you use

It sounds really obvious, but think about where you use your energy, water and resources, and how you could be more efficient.

Consider resource use, climate change and waste. To tackle climate change:

- save energy at home – 'turn down, switch off, unplug'
- buy energy-efficient products – look for the Energy Saving Recommended label or a European energy label rating of A

An energy rating
label for a
washing machine

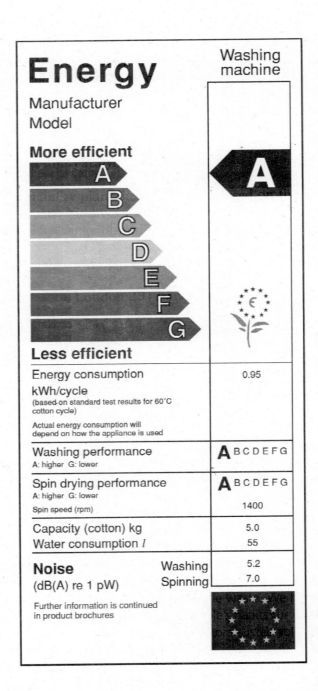

- switch to an energy supplier with a lower carbon footprint or a renewable energy tariff
- improve your home insulation
- try to reduce your car use – walking, cycling or taking the bus or train will help reduce local air pollution and climate change

- tackle the environmental impact of flying by considering options for reducing your travel – for example taking fewer, longer breaks if possible instead of several short ones, holidaying in your home country or travelling to nearby countries by rail or sea. At work, consider video-conferencing rather than travelling long distances for meetings
- consider food miles and low-carbon products
- review your footprint and action plan at www.actonco2.co.uk.

To reduce water use:

- turn off taps properly and fix them if they leak
- install water-efficient products – low flush volume toilets, water-efficient shower heads and aerating heads on washbasin taps help to reduce your water use, as does fitting a 'hippo' or other water-saving device
- collect rainwater in water butts and use it for watering your garden.

Driving

We all know we should use our cars less, but what about when we're in them? Is there anything we can do? This advice is provided by the UK Automobile Association.

Before you go

- Regular servicing. Get the car serviced regularly (according to the manufacturer's schedule) to maintain engine efficiency.
- Tyre pressures. Check tyre pressures regularly and before long journeys. Under-inflated tyres create more rolling resistance and so use more fuel. Getting tyre pressures right is important for safety too. Refer to your car's handbook, as pressures will normally have to be increased for heavier loads.
- Lose weight. Extra weight means extra fuel, so if there's stuff in the boot you don't need on the journey take it out and leave it at home.
- Streamline. Roof racks or boxes create extra wind resistance and so increase fuel consumption. If you don't need it take it off; if you do, pack it carefully to reduce the extra drag.
- Don't get lost. Plan unfamiliar journeys to reduce the chance of getting lost.
- Combine short trips. Cold starts are inefficient, so it pays to combine errands such as buying the paper, dropping off the recycling or collecting the kids into one trip rather than making multiple short trips.
- Consider alternatives. If it's a short journey (a couple of miles or so), consider walking or cycling rather than taking the car. Fuel consumption is worse when the engine is cold, and pollution will be greater too until the emissions control system gets up to normal temperature.

On the way

- Leave promptly. Don't start the engine until you're ready to go. This avoids fuel wastage due to unnecessary idling and ensures that the engine warms up as quickly as possible. In winter months, scrape ice off the windows rather than leaving the car idling for a long period to warm up.
- Easy does it. Drive smoothly, accelerate gently and read the road ahead to avoid unnecessary braking.
- Decelerate smoothly. When you have to slow down or stop, decelerate smoothly by releasing the accelerator in good time, leaving the car in gear.
- Rolling. If you can keep the car moving all the time, so much the better. Stopping then starting again uses more fuel than keeping rolling.
- Change up earlier. Change gear as soon as possible without labouring the engine. Try changing up at an engine speed of around 2,000 rpm in a diesel car or around 2,500 rpm in a petrol car. This can make such a difference to fuel consumption that all cars in the future are likely to be fitted with gear shift indicators that light a lamp on the dashboard to indicate the most efficient gear change points.
- Cut down on the air con. Air conditioning increases fuel consumption at low speeds, but at higher speeds the effects are less noticeable. So if it's a hot day it's more economical to open the windows around town and save the air conditioning for high speed driving. Don't leave the air-con on all the time – but you should run it at least once a week throughout the year to maintain the system in good condition.
- Turn it off. Any electrical load increases fuel consumption, so turn off your heated rear windscreen, demister blowers and headlights when you don't need them.
- Stick to the limits. Drive within the speed limit – the faster you go the greater the fuel consumption and the greater the pollution too. According to the Department for Transport driving at 70 mph uses up to 9 per cent more fuel than at 60 mph and up to 15 per cent more than at 50 mph. Cruising at 80 mph can use up to 25 per cent more fuel than at 70 mph (see the figure on the opposite page).
- Don't be idle. If you do get caught in a queue, avoid wasting fuel by turning the engine off if it looks like you could be waiting for more than three minutes.

Consider what you throw away

Tackle waste
Look at what you throw away and consider the 'seven Rs':

- remove
- reduce
- re-use

Fuel savings from
reduced speed

- repair
- recycle
- recover
- responsibility.

Remove. Can you eliminate the waste you create? Take bags with you when you go shopping, rather than using new ones. Consider whether you need a new item – can you repair or modify one you've got already? Think about the quality of the item you buy – how long will it last?

Reduce. Think about what and how much you buy – do you waste some of it?

Re-use. Pass things on to friends, family and charities if you no longer need them.

Repair. Can it be fixed rather than just replaced?

Recycle. Can you give recyclables to support charities? Most councils run doorstep recycling collections for paper, glass and plastics, but local refuse sites often accept many other things, including wood, shoes, textiles and TVs.

Recover. Consider composting – many local councils offer subsidised compost bins or home collection for kitchen and garden waste.

Responsibility. Take ownership of your waste – make sure it doesn't litter the environment.

Tackle your health
PSR isn't just about your impact on others – you need to look after yourself, too. You can make a big difference by:

- tackling your smoking
- reducing your alcohol intake
- eating healthily, eg five portions of fruit and vegetables a day
- taking more exercise
- practising safe sex.

Be smart in the sun by remembering the 'SunSmart' message provided by Cancer Research UK:

Spend time in the shade between 11 and 3
Make sure you never burn
Aim to cover up with a t-shirt, hat and sunglasses
Remember to take extra care with children
Then use factor 15+ sunscreen

Also report mole changes or unusual skin growths promptly to your doctor.

Tackle your community
You can influence your local community by:

- challenging discrimination wherever you find it
- considering action – voluntary work, involvement in pressure groups or standing for election as a local councillor
- treating others as you'd like to be treated yourself
- being an 'agent of change'
- trying to be a net contributor to life in general
- supporting charities.

Tackle your work
In every other chapter of this book except this one, we've intentionally focused on the organisational level. Now you know what is needed, you can start to influence your organisation to take action:

- Recommend a management systems approach such as SA 8000 or ISO 14001 (see Chapter 6). Even if your organisation decides against external certification, you can still apply the framework.
- Develop (or contribute to) a process for setting objectives and targets.

- Review your success. You don't need a fully accredited approach to be able to make more ethically considered decisions.
- Help shape a vision of what type of organisation you'd like to work for and strive to get others to consider how CSR helps meet their aims.
- Develop an implementation plan to establish your CSR impacts, mitigations, monitoring and reporting.
- Encourage your organisation to measure performance and report. Establish key performance indicators for CSR issues.
- Role shift – look at how you can develop your role to include CSR and influence others.
- Tackle issues in your business linked to CSR – social, environmental, supply chain management, ethical trading, fair trade and engagement with all stakeholder groups.

How can PSR affect CSR?

Better organisations have already recognised that it's only through personal behavioural changes that the highest levels of CSR performance will be achieved. Some have proposed and implemented voluntary personal commitments for each member of staff to pledge to meet CSR and sustainability objectives, believing that this will result in a more positive outcome than compelling staff to comply.

Here is an example of a personal action plan, based on one provided by Salford University in Manchester. For more details, see www.ils.salford.ac.uk/governance/sustain/docs/onlinecharter.php.

Sustainability charter for personal action

Your commitment
I am committed to this charter for personal action and will undertake one or more of the actions below.

Please tick as appropriate:

- ❐ Switch off all lights in a single-occupancy or empty office when leaving it for more than an hour. If we all did this, it would save 5 per cent of our overall electric budget.
- ❐ When printing, do you need a hard copy? If so, re-use the back of old paper. For reports, always print double sided and use recycled paper where possible. Last year, the organisation spent £x with paper suppliers – help reduce this next year.
- ❐ When in the office, especially during summer months, check whether you need all the lights on. If we all turned unnecessary lights off, it would save 5 per cent of our overall electric budget.

☐ Find a partner to share your drive to work with each day, cutting down on single car occupancy. This saves you money, and reduces emissions and congestion. Never drive around with your boot full, and never fill your tank to the top – it's a car not a fuel tanker. A full tank is equivalent to an extra passenger in weight.

☐ Where possible, switch off your computer and monitor before leaving the office for the day. If we all did this, it would wipe 10 per cent off our electric energy bill. Small powered equipment, copiers, and printers account for most of our base load [30%].

☐ Use public transport if possible. One day a week can save you money, and society benefits from reduced congestion and emissions.

☐ Report any dripping taps or water leaks to your facilities department. A dripping tap fills a bath of water every week.

☐ Work with your organisation on sustainable development activities in the local community.

☐ Remember the three Rs – reduce, re-use (plastic carriers, bottles and boxes) and recycle (glass, cans, plastic bottles, paper, computers).

☐ Tell a friend! We need everyone to get involved in this campaign. Remember: not only do we help to save the planet, but all money we save can help to pay for other organisational initiatives, such as enhanced staff benefits or improved and updated equipment.

A possible criticism of this approach is that while the organisation is taking a positive lead, it falls short of requiring staff to meet any set standards. Should the organisation ask staff to volunteer to pledge to and follow these principles, or should it be part of the organisation's mandatory procedures that must be followed? If staff don't choose to make this pledge, what then? However, in the true spirit of CSR, and as each employee is themselves a stakeholder, we need to engage and encourage them to make a difference in their area of responsibility. The idea that 'one volunteer is better than ten pressed men' is a good starting principle from which to help build consensus, and encourages staff to take action where the organisation has no direct control or influence, such as at home.

As an agent for change, you should consider what you have direct influence over. What can you change? Start with yourself, then look around you. Whether or not you decide to start (or continue) taking a CSR approach to your whole life, we've presented this chapter to give you practical ideas to get you thinking about what you can do to become a more socially responsible individual.

The problem is that, as with Newton's third law of motion, every action has an equal and opposite reaction. For everything we buy, use and throw away, we alter the balance of the earth's resources. The question is to what extent we as individuals are willing to compromise our present desires for society and future generations.

PSR is only a start, but it should bring significant benefits to you, your family and your community. After all, everything you do affects everything and everyone else – 'no man is an island'.

> We have changed our environment more quickly than we know how to change ourselves.
> *Walter Lippman (1889–1974), American writer*

Chapter 10: London 2012 – CSR in the future

"Citius, altius, fortius" (Swifter, higher, stronger)
Olympic motto

"When a man is tired of London, he is tired of life; for there is in London all that life can afford."
Samuel Johnson (1709–1784), English author and lexicographer

While an ancient Greek myth tells of the Olympic Games being founded by Hercules, son of Zeus and king of the gods, the earliest written documents of the earthly games tell that a single event, the 'stade' – a run of approximately 192 metres – was held as part of a religious festival to Zeus. The records, dating back to 776 BC, detail the first Olympic champion as Coroebus, who, along with all the other athletes, completed the event naked. These games were accompanied by a truce, allowing Greek Olympians to travel between warring city states in a time of conflict. The popularity of the original games continued to grow, being held every four years for nearly 1,200 years, until they were outlawed by the Roman emperor Theodosius I, a Christian, who abolished the games because of their pagan influences. (IOC, 2008).

The competitive arena of the ancient Greek games held in the 8th century BC may seem a strange place to start the last chapter of this book. The idea of being the best in a gladiatorial battle, of excelling in a competitive event, of being swifter, higher and stronger that your adversaries, would not appear the natural home for altruistic gestures and the ideals and concepts of CSR that we've already covered. But on closer inspection, the concept of fair play and sportsmanship that is quintessential to the Olympic spirit mirrors the philosophy of CSR. As we saw in earlier chapters, CSR is about playing by the rules, not exploiting others, and reaping the rewards in the long run. In sport, only by beating your competitors fairly and within the rules can you leave no room for doubt that you're a world-class athlete, the best in your field and a worthy champion.

In this chapter, we'll look at how the Olympic organisation has become an exemplar in trying to incorporate CSR into its own core goals. We'll also discuss how your organisation could incorporate the sustainability goals of the Olympic Delivery Authority, either to help in winning direct tenders or to use the example of the games to make the changes in your business that will build a legacy of success for many years to come.

Approximately 2,500 years after the first Greek games, a Frenchman named Pierre de Coubertin began the modern Olympic Movement, which established the modern games. The games of the first Olympiad were held in 1896 in Athens, with nine events. The games were always intended to be more than a pure quest for sporting excellence, as shown through the original goal of the Olympic Movement:

> ... to contribute to building a peaceful and better world by educating youth through sport practised without discrimination of any kind and in the Olympic spirit, which requires mutual understanding with a spirit of friendship, solidarity and fair play.
> (IOC, 2008)

This goal has been developed over the intervening century and incorporated into six principles of Olympism that follow the concepts of CSR and PSR.

1. Olympism is a philosophy of life, exalting and combining in a balanced whole the qualities of body, will and mind. Blending sport with culture and education, Olympism seeks to create a way of life based on the joy of effort, the educational value of good example and respect for universal fundamental ethical principles.
2. The goal of Olympism is to place sport at the service of the harmonious development of man, with a view to promoting a peaceful society concerned with the preservation of human dignity.
3. The Olympic Movement is the concerted, organised, universal and permanent action, carried out under the supreme authority of the International Olympic Committee, of all individuals and entities who are inspired by the values of Olympism. It covers the five continents. It reaches its peak with the bringing together of the world's athletes at the great sports festival, the Olympic Games. Its symbol is five interlaced rings.
4. The practice of sport is a human right. Every individual must have the possibility of practising sport, without discrimination of any kind and in the Olympic spirit, which requires mutual understanding with a spirit of friendship, solidarity and fair play. The organisation, administration and management of sport must be controlled by independent sports organisations.
5. Any form of discrimination with regard to a country or a person on grounds of race, religion, politics, gender or otherwise is incompatible with belonging to the Olympic Movement.
6. Belonging to the Olympic Movement requires compliance with the Olympic Charter and recognition by the IOC.

IOC Olympic Charter (2007), www.olympic.org

These principles have been transferred into the host city selection process. Hosting the games is a costly venture, and only if long-term legacy planning maximises the benefits can a worthwhile return be seen on the investment.

London 2012

London 2012 represents an opportunity for the whole of the UK not only to be associated with the games, but to capture the essence of the Olympic ideal. At the core of the London bid was (and is) the concept of legacy, and this is now driving CSR and a programme of sustainable development as part of the delivery of the Olympic event. The construction phase, the games themselves and the legacy give an opportunity to the UK to tackle issues such as sustainable construction, climate change, waste management, social inclusion, obesity and community cohesion. Those who see the games only as a sporting event miss the core values of the Olympic Movement.

The Olympic Delivery Authority (ODA) has developed a sustainability plan that invites those who want to be involved to be more inspired on sustainability issues to act to make a difference, as illustrated in this extract:

Making a real difference
We want to use the Games to illustrate the capacity of major events to influence behaviour and develop knowledge.

We want the Games to inspire people to:
- Recycle more
- Use more public transport, walk and cycle more
- Lifestyle choices – preferences for environmentally efficient homes/work places, sustainable food, and/or greener products…
- More sustainable corporate practices

After the Games we want people to know more about:
- New methods of environmental management, monitoring and reporting
- Demonstration of new, 'green' technology
- Development of 'green' businesses

We also want to use the Games to showcase the sustainable approach and influence the way future major events are managed.
ODA, www.london2012.com

The ODA has included legacy planning from day one, as illustrated in the figure on the next page. Your organisation can start to consider its

The ODA legacy plan for London 2012

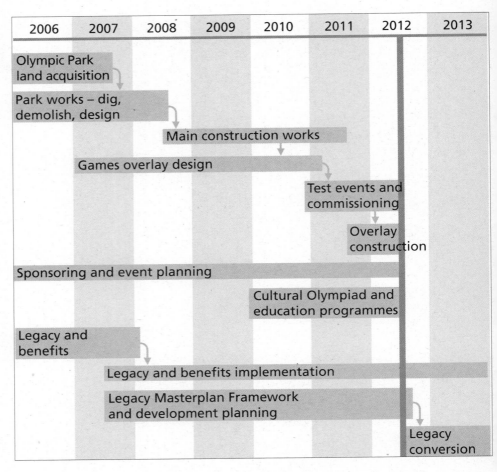

involvement today by considering each of the ODA sustainability plan goals, and using these as drivers for change in your professional and personal life. The 12 key sustainability objectives are:

- minimising carbon emissions
- efficient water use, re-use and recycling
- protecting and enhancing biodiversity
- prioritising walking, cycling and the use of public transport
- optimising the reduction of waste through design
- creating new, safe, mixed-use communities
- environmentally and socially responsible materials
- creating a highly accessible Olympic Park and venues
- optimising land, water and air quality and minimising noise
- creating new employment and business opportunities
- providing healthy lifestyle opportunities
- involving the community.

Clearly, for a publicly funded event to justify spending millions of pounds of taxpayers' money, it has to deliver benefits at many levels. But why should your organisation consider these goals as part of its business objectives? Apart from jumping through a metaphorical hoop in order to gain a contract, what's in it for you?

Test your thinking 18

For each of the 12 sustainability objectives, consider the benefits to you, your organisation and your community from pursuing that objective.

A few of the key benefits are:

Minimising carbon emissions

Carbon management and energy efficiency have a range of benefits to the individual and organisation. Reducing use of fuel, electricity and transport will directly save money. In terms of CSR effects, lower carbon emissions collectively across civilisation will help to control the effects of man-made climate change, including sea level change, the frequency of severe storms, the spread of infectious diseases, disruption to food, water and infrastructure, and population movement caused by climate change.

Efficient water use, re-use and recycling

Water management links directly to energy use, so all the benefits and problems above also apply here. Water is a resource for wildlife habitats, and we also need clean drinking water for general use, so the more we waste, the less we as a society have to use on the things we need. Water also costs money and most businesses and an increasing number of domestic customers are charged for the amount they use.

Protecting and enhancing biodiversity

Biodiversity is important as the variety and number of species reflect the genetic health of our ecosystem. As the climate changes, and human needs change, we need a diverse range of species to maintain supplies of essential products of the biosphere, such as oxygen. Biodiversity also provides a genetic resource for medical, agricultural and technological developments for the future. Wildlife, nature reserves and green spaces also have an amenity value.

Prioritising walking, cycling and the use of public transport

For the individual, this can help to reduce transport costs and increase exercise and personal fitness. For business, it means less demand for car parking, and for society it means reduced congestion and less air pollution.

Optimising the reduction of waste through design

If we use resources inefficiently, we're not only wasting the material in question, but we're also increasing the pollution and environmental degradation caused in the extraction, manufacture, transport, packaging and disposal of that material. This affects you as an individual through air pollution and land contamination from landfill; it affects your organisation since it not only has to buy the materials you throw away but must also pay to dispose of them; and it affects the community, which has to provide landfill, incineration and recycling facilities.

Creating new, safe, mixed-use communities

We all want to live in safety. We can't create all-new communities, but we can all do more to support the community we live in. As individuals, supporting and engaging in our community – by helping a neighbour or supporting voluntary work – brings a range of benefits including personal satisfaction, a greater sense of community and a larger social network. For the business, this can bring benefits including increased staff morale, productivity, good publicity and marketing opportunities. Safer communities are more likely to have reduced crime figures, which reduces the costs of neighbourhood policing.

Environmentally and socially responsible materials

Purchasing power is one of the strongest freedoms we have (see Chapter 9). By choosing environmentally and socially responsible materials, we have the ability to change multinational organisations. Why would Tesco stock fair trade coffee or ASDA-Walmart offer organic chocolate if people didn't want to buy them? For the individual, the purchasing decision helps to demonstrate to the world that they're willing to pay for more ethical practices and a better environment, and thus become an agent of change. For the organisation, more environmentally friendly products and materials may be cheaper in the long run, will increase your energy security, could open new markets and offer a competitive advantage.

Creating highly accessible venues and access to services

According to the Department for Work and Pensions, there are 10 million adults covered by the Disability Discrimination Act (DWP, 2008). For someone with a disability, getting access to your organisation's services brings the simple benefit of being able to interact in society as an able-bodied person can. For your organisation, it brings the benefit of a market of an additional £80 billion (the estimated annual purchasing power of people with disabilities, Family Resources Survey 2002/03), along with the possibility of access to committed and skilled employees, and avoiding court actions for discrimination. For society, the more the barriers to disability are removed, the easier it is for individuals to contribute to the community.

Optimising land, water and air quality and minimising noise

If we optimise land, water and air quality, individuals will benefit from a higher standard of living through less pollution. This reduces the risk of pollution-related medical conditions (such as asthma), causes less stress from noise, and creates a more pleasant environment in which to live. Organisations benefit from not paying for waste or raw materials they don't need, and society will benefit from lower healthcare costs.

Creating new employment and business opportunities

New employment and business opportunities help individuals become more affluent, have greater job satisfaction and improve their standard of living. Organisations can thrive, grow and become more profitable, and therefore pay higher taxes to support community programmes.

Providing healthy lifestyle opportunities

A commitment to healthy lifestyles links educating staff about choosing good diets and taking more regular exercise to managing health and safety at work. For the individual, a healthy lifestyle will reduce the risk of illness (such as heart disease, cancer and diabetes) and improve their length and quality of life, while health and safety at work will reduce the likelihood of work-related disability. Organisations benefit as staff have fewer accidents, are off sick less often and have fewer work-related health problems. This supports the retention of skills and experience within the organisation, reduces civil and criminal liabilities, and increases productivity and profitability. In society, lower rates of illness will lead to more revenue from taxation, lower incapacity benefit payments, less of a burden on the national healthcare service and more productivity – this in turn contributes to a higher GDP.

Involving the community

A community is a collective of consenting individuals. The basic premise of CSR is to run your organisation in a way that does not exploit the individuals, society or environment it comes into contact with. Involving communities benefits the participating individuals through social networking, a sense of achievement and support. The organisation benefits from good public relations, a higher media profile and improved staff morale, and society benefits from increased inputs, such as taxation.

As we have seen, many of the ODA's sustainability objectives could bring tangible benefits to you, your organisation and your community. All the organisations in the London 2012 Olympic supply chain will be required to contribute towards these goals. Organisations which are not involved may be at a distinct disadvantage as they may not have the same competitive edge, and may have less motivated staff with higher sickness absence rates, lower productivity and retention rates, and be less profitable. As intended, the Olympics will 'raise the bar'. Is your organisation training now to achieve gold?

An interesting question for the future is how the ODA will deliver these sustainability objectives while meeting the concurrent objective of hosting successful Olympic and Paralympic Games.

Within the sustainability plan, the ODA has focused on five key themes of climate change, waste, biodiversity, healthy living and inclusion. In each area, it has planned a range of initiatives to help minimise its environmental impact and maximise the social and economic benefits in the construction, event and legacy phases.

This extract is from the London 2012 Sustainability Plan:

Climate change

As far as possible, we will ensure that everything that is being constructed can be used and improved on in the future. For example, we are planning so that the communities that remain in and around the Olympic Park after the Games will be able to access local renewable energy sources as new, low/zero carbon fuels become available.

After the Games, at least 20 per cent of energy requirements will be supplied by on-site renewable energy sources.

The close proximity of the Park to transport connections and the creation of new footpaths and cycle routes will help reduce car dependency among the local community.

Waste

Through the education campaigns we run before and during the Games, we will encourage people to reduce, reuse or recycle waste. We hope that the 2012 programme will aim to help change people's habits for good – and inspire other major events in the future to be more sustainable.

The Games will act as a catalyst for the development of new waste processing facilities in east London which will provide a lasting facility.

Biodiversity

The Olympic Park Masterplan provides for 102 hectares of open space. The Park will be the largest new urban green space in Europe and the area will benefit from:

- enhanced water and land habitats;
- open water and wetlands; and
- species-rich grasslands.

The types of plant used will be native to south-east England (and ideally of locally-grown stock), which are suited to predicted future climates. This will help the whole site be better adapted to climate change, through its ability to cope with heavy rainfall events as well as providing greenery to provide shade.

Healthy living

The legacy of a new parkland designed to promote walking, cycling and provide sporting facilities for the elite athletes and the community has excellent health benefits for the area. In addition, permanent buildings will be converted into service buildings that will support the community. These include:

- the Aquatics Centre will be available for use by local residents; and
- the Polyclinic (which will offer medical services to athletes during the Games) will be transformed by Newham Primary Care Trust into a new primary care centre for local people.

Sport programmes will continue to be developed as a result of the London 2012 Games across London and the UK.

Inclusion

To make London 2012 'everyone's Games', the UK Government and the Mayor of London have prepared delivery plans to ensure that benefits and participation can be spread as widely as possible. The Government published 'Our Promise for 2012' in June 2007, and is planning to publish a detailed legacy action plan in 2008.

The Mayor published 'Your 2012' summarising its delivery plans, in July 2007.

London 2012 is committed to working closely with local authorities and communities, in order to maximise the benefits that the Park can deliver after the Games, in terms of:

- re-integrating communities on either side of the Lower Lea Valley;
- creating housing (including affordable housing) and jobs for local people;
- creating parkland and legacy venues that will benefit local communities, as well as supporting elite sports; and
- enabling social cohesion, and social, economic and environmental regeneration in one of the most underdeveloped parts of the UK.

London 2012 Sustainability Plan, www.london2012.com

The Olympic Games are unique. Every organisation needs to look at its own social, economic and environmental impacts and develop an appropriate CSR management programme to maximise the benefits to its stakeholders.

Test your thinking 19

We'd like you now to consider the five key themes of the ODA's sustainability plan. How does your organisation affect its stakeholders in these areas? What CSR action could your organisation take to optimise the benefits in these five theme areas?

- climate change
- waste
- biodiversity
- healthy living
- inclusion.

Here are some possible answers and 34 ideas for action.

Climate change – 10 ideas
- Identify all sources of direct and indirect greenhouse gas releases from your organisation's operations. Consider electricity use, direct burning of fossil fuels (eg mains gas boilers) and other releases of greenhouse gases, eg air conditioner refrigerants, transport.
- Measure and establish monitoring methods for each of your releases, and establish a benchmark from which improvements can be verified.
- Turn off anything not in use or on standby.
- Help your staff to grasp the issues with posters, emails and briefings.
- Change your energy supplier to one with a renewable tariff or with a lower carbon dioxide generation mix.
- Research best practice – visit the Carbon Trust website (www.carbontrust.co.uk) for support and information.
- Buy energy-efficient equipment and include energy use as a criterion in your purchasing policy.
- Promote energy efficiency among your suppliers.
- Develop your processes and products to be more energy-efficient.
- After reducing your energy use, consider carbon offsetting (see the figure on the next page).

Waste – 10 ideas
- Classify all your waste streams, establishing what is produced, how much there is of it and where it's currently disposed of. This could be linked to an awareness programme, such as 'record what you bin today'.

Stage 1: Direct emissions reduction	Stage 2: Indirect emissions reduction	Stage 3: Offsetting
▶ Calculate emissions	▶ Map supply chain process	▶ Establish reasons for buying offsets
▶ Look for internal abatement opportunities	▶ Identify opportunities for emissions reduction	▶ Define type of offsets to be bought
▶ Develop an emissions reduction/carbon management plan	▶ Develop an implementation plan across the supply chain	▶ Carry out due diligence on robustness of offsets
	▶ Bring new low-carbon products to market	

The Carbon Trust three-stage approach to developing robust offsetting strategy

- Establish regular monitoring for each waste stream. Calculate the annual waste footprint, including the amount sent for recycling or landfill. Include this in management reports and information to staff, including the cost of waste disposal and the items being disposed of, if possible.
- Review legal compliance requirements in relation to the waste management duty of care, including controlled and hazardous waste, waste electrical and electronic equipment, and packaging.
- Get commitment from key influencers, appoint champions and set targets to aim for. Develop action plans to implement waste minimisation or reduction measures and assign responsibilities.
- Investigate waste reduction options. Review all of your organisation's processes – start with packaging waste. Also consider your purchasing policy so that you can be sure that you're buying the correct stock to prevent waste in the first place.
- Review your processes. Consider lean production and quality control principles, such as smaller batch sizes to reduce the amount of waste you create.
- Consider your outputs. Is your product as energy-efficient, minimally packaged and eco-designed as it could be?
- From the thorough process review in ideas 5, 6 and 7, apply the waste hierarchy (see the figure on the next page) in relation to each waste stream. Ask these questions in turn:
  ◦ can the waste be eliminated completely?
  ◦ can the volume, weight or hazardous content be reduced?
  ◦ can the item be re-used or repaired either in house or by others?
  ◦ can the material be recycled?
  ◦ are you using licensed carriers and disposal methods (ie responsible disposal) to get rid of any remaining waste?

The waste
hierarchy

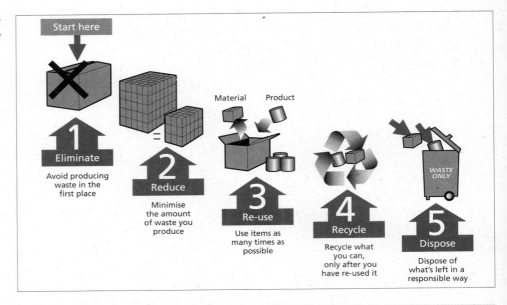

Also consider:
- including waste and recycling monitoring in inspection reports
- contacting suppliers to encourage them to use minimum or returnable packaging
- encouraging paperless systems where feasible
- monitoring ordering amounts and maintaining good stock control
- researching best practice on websites such as WRAP (www.wrap.org.uk) and Envirowise (www.envirowise.gov.uk)
- providing information on how to reduce waste, eg next to printers and photocopiers
- considering product shelf life and disposal methods at the purchasing stage.

- Provide training to staff, and explain how important it is to eliminate, reduce, re-use and recycle. Emphasise the volume and cost of waste, and the cost of replacing the item you're throwing away. Implement a staff suggestion and/or reward scheme.
- Spread the news. Include information on waste recycling schemes, reductions and cost savings in reports, internal communications and company newsletters.

Biodiversity – four ideas
- Consider nature conservation in your procurement policy, and make sure paper and timber is from Forestry Stewardship Council certified sources. Make sure no items you use are on the CITES lists – see Chapter 9 for more details on labelling and markings.

- Consider your landscaped areas, and maximise their wildlife value. Rather than having just mown grass, investigate the possibility of:
  - choosing plant species suitable to the local environment – use native species where suitable
  - planting ground cover in some areas to provide habitat for birds, small mammals and invertebrates
  - planting dense shrubs to provide safe nesting sites, and plants that bear berries to provide food for wildlife
  - choosing plants that flower and fruit in different seasons to create year-round food sources and visual interest
  - selecting nectar-producing varieties of flowering plants and avoid F1 hybrids known not to produce pollen and nectar
  - replanting with native species where non-native trees are due for replacement
  - retaining crevices, slots and holes for invertebrates in wooden fences and on buildings and similar structures
  - reducing use of mowers and leaf clearing machines that remove invertebrates and organic material
  - installing nest boxes and bird baths
  - installing insect nesting boxes in suitable locations
  - reviewing and, if necessary, modifying use of horticultural chemicals
  - using peat-free compost and manure on flower beds
  - using only organic fertilisers
  - providing information boards at the entrances to your grounds explaining what you're doing to improve biological diversity.
  (This list is based on information provided by the Westminster Biodiversity Partnership 'Local Biodiversity Action Plan'.)
- Review pollution and spillage control to ensure the protection of local watercourses, especially those leading to local natural reserves or Sites of Special Scientific Interest.
- Support local nature conservation groups, voluntary workers and wildlife trusts.

Healthy living – five ideas

- Make sure your workplace occupational health management system is implemented as intended.
- Promote offsite health and safety to staff – employees injured at home in DIY or sporting accidents have an impact on your organisation. Consider promotional literature to give staff guidance on good practices.
- Promote a healthy lifestyle through good nutrition and regular exercise. Investigate reduced membership fees for people wanting to use a gym – or open one on site if you have the space and funds.
- Positively support a healthy work–life balance. Staff who are less stressed are more productive, take less time off work and will stay in their job

longer. Review the kinds of flexible work patterns that are feasible for your organisation. Respond positively when your staff ask for flexibility.
- Provide supportive information: this could be leaflets or web addresses of groups to help with childcare, debt relief or benefits, or more resource-intensive initiatives, such as providing a counselling and employee assistance programme (sometimes known as an 'EAP'), or private health care.

Inclusion – five ideas
- Review the accessibility of your site, seeking external advice if necessary. Consider the needs of customers and employees.
- Review your recruitment, promotion and retention policies. Consider where you advertise, what skills or abilities are actually needed for the job, and whether the current policies reflect best practice and legal standards.
- Review your products and services. How do they meet the needs of people with disabilities or individuals from a range of social backgrounds? Is there an opportunity to develop the product or service to gain access to these markets?
- Consider open days and educational activities to support local schools, and give talks or work experience opportunities.
- Support the rehabilitation of staff following long-term absence.

Beyond the Olympics
The Olympics have always embodied the ideal of Olympic virtue and the CSR principle of being the best you can be (without this being at the expense of others). This ideal is not new; consider the Victorian philanthropists who saw that social reforms, such as relocating workers to out-of-town developments, benefited not only workers but business as well. Accordingly, their legacy formed companies such as Cadbury's, Rowntree and Lloyds Bank (see Chapter 2).

It's clear that social reform isn't a new business concept. In an environmentally aware, image-conscious and global market, the stakes are higher than ever. In this chapter, we've reviewed in some depth how your organisation could follow the Olympic ideal for CSR: you should aim to be swifter at meeting the needs of your stakeholders, reach higher to be more successful and be a stronger organisation to overcome the pressures that lie ahead.

But what about after 2012? Is CSR just 'the new black' – just another fashion?

Two hundred and four National Olympic Committees participated in the opening ceremony of the Beijing Olympic Games in 2008. With every nation having many organisations that affect and are affected by CSR, it's more than probable that responsible competitiveness will only continue to grow and evolve as we learn more about the interactions between organisations and the earth and its inhabitants. The importance of responsible competitiveness will continue to present an opportunity for organisations to demonstrate their abilities to stand above the marketplace, and to demonstrate their integrity to their customers.

Pascal Lamy, the Director-General of the World Trade Organization, has this to say:

> Responsible competitiveness is an essential ingredient for effective global markets. It blends forward-looking corporate strategies, innovative public policies, and a vibrant, engaged civil society. It is about creating a new generation of profitable products and business processes underpinned by rules that support societies' broader social, environmental and economic aims.

Summary

Throughout this book, we've encouraged you to look at the many interactions between your organisation and society. As you've worked through the 'Test your thinking' exercises, you'll have realised that organisations are not like islands, standing on their own, but that they have positive and negative impacts on the communities they serve.

Stakeholders of a company can apply a range of pressures which can represent an opportunity for companies but also for individuals.

CSR needs urgently to be extended into the personal sphere, where each of us accepts the true price of the goods and services we buy, and the broader impacts of the purchasing decisions we make.

If we expect companies to take CSR seriously, consumers need to drive the market. Only then will organisations see the opportunity that CSR represents. As a result, business and society will get the benefits of a more ethical, less environmentally damaging, more socially focused economic system, with the potential to give everyone better quality of life.

Endnote

We genuinely hope that you've enjoyed reading about CSR and PSR, and testing your own thinking as you've progressed. We want you to do something for the earth right now. Believe that you personally can make a difference. We're worried that humans have become a parasite that's about to kill its host. There's nothing at all extraordinary in earth's history about extinctions of species. Drastic and immediate action is needed. Every journey starts with a single step, and today is your day to take that first step. Good luck in all that you do to help us all.

One small step for man, one giant leap for mankind
Astronaut Neil Armstrong, 20 July 1969, from the surface of the Moon

Appendix 1: 100 CSR actions

Here is a ready-to-go list of possible CSR-related actions that you could get started on right away. Together, these comprise a programme of activities to help your organisation to quickly and substantially improve its credentials. Of course, no list can be absolutely definitive, and we welcome comments and suggestions from readers. These, where appropriate, will be included and credited in future editions of this book.

Management
1. Always start at work by seeking support for your ideas from management. (Almost) anything can be achieved with senior support.
2. Draft and adopt a CSR policy for your organisation. We've included an example in Appendix 2. Feel free to use it, amend it to suit your own requirements and communicate it to all members of staff. Keep records of everything you do under the policy.
3. Identify your key stakeholders. Let them know what you're doing. Assess their interest, and tell them your broad intentions. Staff and customers (and possibly others) will ask questions. Be ready to answer their questions promptly.
4. Conduct a baseline review. Use the guidance in this book to identify the significant CSR-related impacts in your organisation.
5. Prioritise your initial action plan. Focus on (say) five main issues, and set objectives and shorter-term milestone targets.
6. Implement your plans. Keep on top of changing circumstances, and the changing expectations of your stakeholders.
7. Promote CSR in your supply chain. Suggest to your suppliers and clients that they may want to join you on your journey.
8. Monitor progress, perhaps against appropriate performance indicators.
9. Make sure that top management is involved in a regular senior review – say six-monthly or annually.
10. Decide whether external certification (eg ISO 14001, SA 8000) is appropriate.

Community
11. Think of ways to engage with the organisation's neighbours – the people who live nearby. For example, hold an open day or invite them to a 'town hall meeting'.
12. Consider and write down your organisation's impacts on the local labour market and the local environment.
13. Be ready to provide external support to the local and regional community (when you can) following loss of essential services such as water or electricity.

14. Select a charity of the year and help with fundraising activities for it. Perhaps the organisation could match the funds raised by staff?

15. Tell your staff that you'll provide an agreed amount of time to support voluntary and charitable organisations. How about a volunteer scheme, say one day per employee per year to provide your organisation's specialist skills? How about reading mentoring to a local school? Or work placement?

16. Look again at your purchasing policy. Are the payment terms and cancellation charges as fair as they should be?

17. Promote car sharing. Offer incentives and benefits (convenient parking spaces, leave five minutes earlier), or make small donations in kind to a nominated charity.

18. Support local teams – football, cricket, Scouts, Brownies.

19. Buy from local vendors.

20. Prepare a regular newsletter and circulate it widely. Good communications are an important part of any new initiative. And you'll soon have good news to share.

Environment

21. Always prevent pollution. Tell staff how important this is, whether it's litter or an oil slick.

22. Purchase recycled, low-energy, low-environmental impact equipment. Look for the energy labelling. And return electrical equipment to the store where you bought it when it's no longer usable.

23. Reduce, re-use, recycle.

24. Promote environmental initiatives among your staff.

25. Measure your carbon footprint. Reduce what you can, offset what you can't reduce. Offsetting your carbon footprint isn't expensive.

26. Always be on the lookout for leaks. Include this on inspection checklists and site tours. Minimise leaks of water and from air lines, as well as spills.

27. Develop an emergency plan for foreseeable losses. This will help a lot if things go wrong. And don't forget to practise so that you're sure the plan works reliably.

28. Sort out a transport policy for the organisation. Minimise unnecessary trips, plan for return loads and help drivers with route-planning. Set out your organisation's long-term vision, and discuss it with your staff.

29. Include hybrid cars in the fleet and avoid 'gas guzzlers'.

30. Don't use or buy anything included on the CITES list (endangered wild animals and plants).

Ethics

31. Review your employment policies, specifically looking for any form of discrimination.
32. Establish fair grievance procedures.
33. Develop and publish an ethical procurement policy.
34. Invest in ethical funds.
35. Make clear to all your staff that bribery and corruption in any form are completely unacceptable. We suggest that you give relevant examples of unacceptable practices – eg entertainment, gifts, financial inducements.
36. Don't engage in any anti-competitive practices (anti-trust). Take legal advice if necessary.
37. Vow never to take advantage in times of crisis (eg if you sell generators, don't increase the price when there's a power cut).
38. Consult as early as possible as market conditions change, eg with employees and suppliers.
39. Take all steps necessary to confirm there is no child labour in your supply chain.
40. Take responsibility for your actions in the marketplace. We suggest the following examples make great starting points:
    - pay suppliers according to the terms you've agreed
    - undertake responsible labelling and marketing
    - acknowledge patents, property and copyright
    - pay a fair rate for work, goods and services
    - recall defective products promptly.

Human rights

41. Take all steps necessary to confirm there is no facilitation of illegal labour, and no bonded labour or slavery in your supply chain.
42. Audit and review your business practices and premises for access for people with disabilities – it's the law!
43. Promote life-long learning and continual development among your staff.
44. Maintain a policy of equal pay for equal work.
45. Support staff who want to participate in civic duties, eg as elected councillors, special constables, members of the Territorial Army.
46. Treat people who complain about your products or services with respect. Investigate the problem and understand their point of view.
47. Support staff who may be victimised, eg because of educational difficulties, their sexuality or disabilities.
48. Actively fight racism, inform staff of your company policy, and don't let racist comments go unchallenged.
49. Don't tell discriminatory jokes – and don't forward them.
50. Don't buy counterfeit products that indirectly support illegal practices.

Workforce

51. Communicate with your workforce transparently, promptly and accurately.
52. Moderate your expectations for working hours – employees have lives outside work!
53. Consider the feasibility of flexitime and family-friendly polices.
54. Conduct regular staff development reviews.
55. Workers generally come to work to do their best, but they'll sometimes make mistakes. Recognise this, and be humane with them when they do.

At home

56. Turn TVs and other electrical items off – don't leave them on standby.
57. Fit energy-efficient light bulbs.
58. Insulate your home, block drafts and close off unused rooms.
59. Choose a fuel-efficient vehicle (consider a bicycle).
60. Use public transport where possible.
61. Live near where you work – don't over-commute. This way, you'll see more of your family, too.
62. Consider the impact of your holidays on the environment.
63. Turn the tap off when you brush your teeth.
64. Talk to your kids about CSR – it's in the UK National Curriculum!
65. Improve biodiversity in your garden. Plant native species, keep woody offcuts where possible to encourage wildlife and try not to use too many chemicals.
66. Grow your own vegetables (zero food miles!).
67. Eat more vegetarian meals – meat takes more greenhouse gases, land, water and chemicals to produce.
68. Boycott bottled water – drink tap water.
69. Take showers, not baths.
70. Re-use shopping bags.

PSR – personal social responsibility

71. Consider what you buy.
72. Consider what you use.
73. Tackle climate change – look at your energy consumption.
74. Tackle water use.
75. Tackle your car – consider alternative transport if possible.
76. Tackle your driving.
77. Consider what you throw away.
78. Tackle your health.
79. Tackle your community.
80. Tackle your work.

Health and safety at work

81. Comply with the law on health, safety and welfare. If you operate in more than one country, apply common standards based on the highest requirements. And if there's no legal requirement in your territory, look to the United Kingdom – it's been regulating for over 200 years!

82. Undertake assessments to confirm that workplace risks have been reduced to tolerable levels.

83. Support consultation through safety representatives. Make joint inspections of the workplace, and investigate every accident and near miss reported. Deal promptly with the issues that come up.

84. Manage contractors as though they were your own staff. Never sub-contract 'hazardous work' for only that reason.

85. 50,000 drivers die on the roads of Europe each year, and thousands more elsewhere. Promote road safety, and provide enhanced training and safe, well-maintained vehicles to drivers.

86. Consider behavioural safety programmes – a positive and inclusive way to reduce accidents.

87. Encourage employees to 'take health and safety home' – eg initiatives to promote safe DIY.

88. Promote healthy eating. If you have a works canteen, offer healthy options on every menu.

89. AIDS and other sexually transmitted diseases are prevalent in many parts of the world. Make sure staff are aware of the risks when they travel.

90. Develop a rehabilitation programme to maintain work wellness, and help sick or injured employees to return to work. Stress (in particular) is on the increase, and employers should be prepared.

General

91. Be informed. Re-read this book, and use the contacts and links within it. Use the internet to research your subject – it changes rapidly, and it pays to keep up to date. Have a look at our 'Websites to watch' section on page 141.

92. Get active. Join a group which promotes something you believe in. It could be a wildlife charity, an environmental pressure group, or a political party.

93. Publicly promote CSR and your values, write articles, give speeches and pass on the word – explain the benefits to others.

94. Consider benchmarking your organisation against others to see if your standards meet up to best practice.

95. Get involved in your sector's trade association working group on CSR. If there isn't one, consider setting one up.

96. Develop a register for your legal requirements for employment, health and safety and environmental law, and regularly review compliance.
97. Review the feasibility of becoming accredited to the Investor in People standard.
98. Consider using the SEDEX supplier database for international suppliers to verify standards and minimise their administrative burden – www.sedex.org.uk.
99. Review your process for investing in new projects. Consider the CSR implications at the earliest stage – it's more cost effective.
100. Start today. Take the first step, have faith, believe in your cause and don't give up!

Test your thinking 20

Consider the 100 actions and write down the top 10 that you can go and implement today.

Appendix 2: Sample CSR policy

Each organisation's CSR issues will vary and, of course, the policy and strategy you adopt should reflect this. Your policy should demonstrate the commitment of senior management, clarify the main issues that the organisation is to tackle and provide a platform for implementation, checking and review.

This sample policy will help you make a start.

Sample CSR policy

Our organisation recognises that it operates in a community, society and world that we all share. We are committed to continually improving our operations and performance to minimise our negative impacts and maximise our positive effects on the communities we interact with. We believe that our corporate social responsibility policy plays a vital role in the success of our operations. To this end we will:

1. comply with all relevant national laws and international agreements applicable to the countries we operate in
2. engage with our stakeholders, listen to their concerns and strive to eliminate or mitigate our negative impacts
3. treat the workforce with respect, upholding labour rights and actively supporting human rights throughout our supply chain
4. minimise risk to our workforce, those who use our products, and the communities who may be affected by our operations
5. drive ethical trading principles throughout our organisation and supply chain
6. challenge bribery and corruption
7. develop the life cycle of our products and services to minimise their impact on the environment, and support sustainable development
8. support the communities we operate in.

We have developed a corporate social responsibility strategy to embed these principles into our organisation, and have implemented a management framework to regularly monitor, audit and review our progress, to drive change and challenge convention. This policy will be communicated to our stakeholders and will be followed by our staff and all those who work on our behalf.

Signed
Position
Date

References

Asbury S W. A risk-based approach to auditing. *The Environmentalist* June 2005; 29.

Asbury S W and Ashwell P. *Health and safety, environment and quality audits – a risk-based approach*. Elsevier, 2007.

British Airports Authority. *Sustainable construction at Terminal 5*. Business in the Community, 2002.

Brundtland G H. *Our common future: report of the World Commission on Environment and Development*. United Nations World Commission on Environment and Development, 1987.

Dalrymple G B. *The age of the earth*. Stanford University Press, 1991.

Darwin C. *On the origin of species by means of natural selection, or the preservation of favoured races in the struggle for life*. John Murray, 1859.

Department for Food, the Environment and Rural Affairs. *Taking forward the UK Climate Change Bill: the government response to pre-legislative scrutiny and public consultation*. HMSO, 2007.

Devalia A and Instone A. *Personal social responsibility: a powerful workbook for being socially responsible in business*. Nirvana Publishing, 2008.

Department for Work and Pensions. Family resources survey, www.dwp.gov.uk/asd/frs, 2008.

Environment Agency. Sustainable procurement guide, www.environment-agency.gov.uk/commondata/103599/spg_517077.doc, 2006.

Fastovsky D E and Sheehan P M. The extinction of the dinosaurs in North America. *GSA Today* 2005: 15 (3): 4–10.

Holme R and Watts P. *Making good business sense*. World Business Council for Sustainable Development, 2000.

Health and Safety Executive. *The cost of accidents at work* (HSG96). HSE Books, 1997.

International Finance Corporation. *Stakeholder engagement: a good practice handbook for companies doing business in emerging markets*. World Bank Group, 2008.

International Olympic Committee. See www.olympic.org.uk/index.asp.

King L W. *The code of Hammurabi*. Kessinger Publishing, 2004.

Klein N. *No Logo*. Picador, 2000.

Schanberg S H. On the playgrounds of America, every kid's goal is to score. In Pakistan, where children stitch soccer balls for six cents an hour, the goals is to survive. *Life Magazine* June 1996: 38–48

Medvedev G. *The truth about Chernobyl*. Basic Books, 1991.

More E and Webley S. *Does business ethics pay? Ethics and financial performance*. Institute of Business Ethics, 2003.

MORI. *Winning the integrity*. MORI, 2000.

Office for National Statistics. Family Resources Survey 2002/03. See www.statistics.gov.uk/ssd/surveys/survey_family_resources.asp.

Parker G. *The Times atlas of world history*. Times Books, 1997.

Raup D M. *Extinction: bad genes or bad luck?* W W Norton and Co., 1991.

Spodek H. *The world's history: combined volume*. Prentice Hall, 2001.

Office for National Statistics. Statistics 2008, www.statistics.gov.uk.

Stuart G S and Stuart G E. Lost Kingdoms of the Maya. National Geographic Society, 1993.

United Nations. Global Forest Resources Assessment, 2005.

Wells H G. *Outline of history: volume one*. MacMillan, 1920.

Wilson E O. *The future of life*. Knopf, 2002.

World Conservation Union. Convention on International Trade in Endangered Species of Wild Fauna and Flora, 1979. See www.cites.org.

Bibliography

Allchin R (ed). *The archaeology of early historic South Asia: the emergence of cities and states*. Cambridge University Press, 1995.

Baines J and Malek J. *The cultural atlas of Ancient Egypt* (revised edition). Checkmark Books, 2000.

Bard K A. *Encyclopedia of the archaeology of Ancient Egypt*. Routledge, 1999.

Bellwood P. *First farmers: the origins of agricultural societies*. Blackwell, 2004.

Blainey G. *A short history of the world*. Penguin, 2000.

Brady J (ed.). *Environmental management in organizations: the IEMA handbook*. Earthscan, 2005.

Burckhardt J (trans. Middlemore S G C). *The civilization of the Renaissance in Italy*. Penguin, 1990.

Chakrabarti D K. *Indus civilization sites in India: new discoveries*. Marg Publications, 2004.

Cohen M N. *The food crisis in prehistory: overpopulation and the origins of agriculture*. Yale University Press, 1977.

Crawford O G S. Antiquity. Antiquity Publications, 1927.

Dani A H and Mohen J-P (eds). *History of humanity. Volume III: From the third millennium to the seventh century BC*. Routledge/UNESCO, 1996.

Diamond J. *Guns, germs, and steel*. W W Norton and Co., 1999.

Eves D and Gummer J. *Questioning performance: the director's essential guide to health, safety and the environment*. IOSH, 2005.

Global Reporting Initiative. Sustainability reporting guidelines. www.globalreporting.org/home.

Grant E. *The foundations of modern science in the Middle Ages: their religious, institutional, and intellectual contexts*. Cambridge University Press, 1996.

Grimal N. *A history of Ancient Egypt*. Blackwell, 1992.

Gombrich E H. *A little history of the world*. Yale University Press, 2005.

Hallo W W and Simpson W K. *The ancient Near East: a history*. Holt Rinehart and Winston Publishers, 1997.

Hitchcock D and Willard M. *The business guide to sustainability*. Earthscan, 2006.

Hyde P and Reeve P. *Essentials of environmental management* (2nd edition). IOSH, 2004.

Liu H, Prugnolle F, Manica A and Balloux F. A geographically explicit genetic model of worldwide human-settlement history. *The American Journal of Human Genetics* 2006; 79: 230–237.

Institute of Environmental Management and Assessment. *Corporate social responsibility: a guide to good practice*. IEMA, 2007.

McNeill W H. *In the beginning: a world history* (4th edition). Oxford University Press, 1999.

More C. *Understanding the Industrial Revolution*. Routledge, 2000.

Reuters. *The state of the world: the story of the 21st century*. Reuters, 2006.

Rice E F. *The foundations of early modern Europe: 1460–1559*. W W Norton and Co., 1970.

Roddick A. A third way for business, too. *New Statesman* 3 April 1998.

Sasson J. *The civilizations of the ancient Near East*. Scribner, 1995.

Schmandt-Besserat D. Signs of life. *Archaeology Odyssey* Jan–Feb 2002; 6–7: 63.

Musser G. The climax of humanity. *Scientific American* August 2005.

Tudge C. *Neanderthals, bandits and farmers: how agriculture really began*. Weidenfeld & Nicolson, 1998.

United Nations Global Compact Network. The Global Compact. www.unglobalcompact.org.

United Nations Office of the High Commissioner on Human Rights. The International Bill of Human Rights. www.unhchr.ch/html/menu6/2/fs2.htm.

Van de Mieroop M. *History of the ancient Near East: ca. 3000–323 BC*. Blackwell, 2003.

Webster H. *World history*. D C Heath, 1921.

Williams H S. *The historians' history of the world – a comprehensive narrative of the rise and development of nations as recorded by over two thousand of the great writers of all ages*. The Outlook Company, 1904.

Websites to watch

AccountAbility: www.accountability21.net
Business for Social Responsibility: www.bsr.org
Business in the Community: www.bitc.org.uk
Business Link CSR pages: www.businesslink.gov.uk/bdotg/action/
    layer?topicID=1075408468
Convention on International Trade in Endangered Species (CITES):
    www.cites.org
CORE – the corporate responsibility coalition: www.corporate-
    responsibility.org
CorpWatch – holding corporations accountable: www.corpwatch.org
CSR newswire: www.csrwire.com
Employers' Forum on Disability: www.efd.org.uk
Envirowise: www.envirowise.gov.uk
European business network for CSR: www.csreurope.org
Global Reporting Initiative: www.globalreporting.org
Institute of Environmental Management and Assessment: www.iema.net
Institution of Occupational Safety and Health: www.iosh.co.uk
Mallen Baker – CSR news and resources: www.mallenbaker.net
McSpotlight – pressure group on big business: www.mcspotlight.org
Mind Tools – a selection of mind-mapping exercises: www.mindtools.com
Olympic Delivery Authority for the London 2012 Olympics:
    www.london2012.com
UK Department for Business, Enterprise and Regulatory Reform CSR
    pages: www.berr.gov.uk/whatwedo/sectors/sustainability/
    corp-responsibility/page45192.html
UK Environment Agency: www.environment-agency.gov.uk
UK government CSR website: www.csr.gov.uk
UN Environmental Programme: www.unep.org
UN Global Compact: www.unglobalcompact.org/AbouttheGC/
    TheTENPrinciples/index.html
World Business Council for Sustainable Development: www.wbcsd.org/
    templates/TemplateWBCSD5/layout.asp?MenuID=1
WRAP – Material change for a better environment: www.wrap.org.uk

Index